C000280707

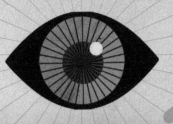

ANGELS
DAVID GRANT

Activities by

Esmonde Banks
and Laura Russell

PEARSON

Heinemann is an imprint of Pearson Education Limited, Edinburgh Gate, Harlow, Essex, CM20 2JE.

www.heinemann.co.uk

Heinemann is a registered trademark of Pearson Education Limited.

Play text © David Grant 2012
Activities text © Pearson Education 2012
Typeset by Phoenix Photosetting, Chatham, Kent, UK

The right of David Grant to be identified as author of this work has been asserted by him in accordance with the Copyright, Designs and Patents Act 1988.

First published 2012

16 15 14 13
11 10 9 8 7 6 5 4 3 2

British Library Cataloguing in Publication Data
A catalogue record for this book is available from the British Library.

ISBN 9780435082857

Printed in China (CTPS/02)

To find out more about David Grant go to www.davidgrantwriter.co.uk

Contents

Teaching resources

To help deliver the questions and activities on pages 86–98, teaching materials are available to download free from www.heinemann.co.uk/literature

---

Introduction

The Stanford Prison Experiment

In 1971, Professor Philip Zimbardo organised an experiment to explore the effect of power and authority on ordinary people. He recreated a prison in the basement of the Stanford University psychology building. Seventy university students applied to take part. Those who were found to have psychological or medical problems or a history of crime or drug abuse were rejected. Twenty-four volunteers were selected, randomly divided into two groups and assigned the roles of either prisoners or guards. The guards were given no training and no instructions other than to maintain law, order and the prisoners' respect.

On the second day of the experiment, the prisoners rebelled, blocking their cell doors with their beds and refusing to obey orders. The guards turned fire extinguishers on the prisoners to get them away from the cell doors, then forced their way into the cells, stripped the prisoners naked and placed the rebellion's ringleaders in solitary confinement.

The brutality of some guards grew: prisoners were made to line up outside their cells, call out their prisoner number and be counted over and over again, often in the middle of the night. After sleepless nights, prisoners were then subjected to extreme and repetitive physical exercise. Some prisoners became physically ill as a result; some broke down and cried uncontrollably; one refused to eat.

After six days, the brutality of some guards and the reactions of some prisoners had become so extreme that Professor Zimbardo was forced to stop the experiment. The 24 volunteers who had been carefully tested and identified as normal, intelligent, responsible young men were released from their roles.

Cast list

Students

Jimmy

Jimmy's friends
Ollie
Anika
Jess

In Jimmy's class
Hayley
Harry
Sean
Aidan
Beth
Jade
Bradley
Kyle

In the year below
Amy
Shane
Ed
Nav

Staff

Voice
Voice 1
Voice 2

Staging suggestions

The way that any director or any cast approaches staging a play is bound to be only one way of looking at the text. Even the oldest plays are endlessly reinterpreted as we continue to find new ways of looking at them. Quite simply, there is no right or wrong way to stage a play, but there are ways which offer greater or lesser challenges to actors and audiences. These staging suggestions will depend more on developing a strong ensemble feel within your cast than they will on bulky and costly sets. As a theatre-goer, I feel the drama starts to die the moment a curtain closes and you hear the scenery trundling around, and it can take a long time to regain lost momentum. I always want the story and the characters to keep moving. I think audiences are happy to suspend disbelief and use their own imaginations if you reward them with a performance that has wit, charm, style and vision, even if you are working in a limited or limiting space.

Angels is a gift to any director in one sense: it is a play about ideas, characters and choices rather than places and spaces. The setting can be non-specific and almost no scenery is required; the audience just need to know that the action takes place in a school. A few chairs and desks will be all you need. However, because the setting is consistent throughout the play, you will want to create some visual interest.

Staging

This is a subtle and intimate play, and I think the audience need to feel that they are almost *in the action*. They should get the sense that they are bystanders, watching the tale unfold up close. To create an experience which is as immersive and visually interesting as possible, I suggest the following:

- Approach this piece in the round, performing on the floor rather than a stage.
- Use four aisles which come off the performance area and go

through the audience. This will help to keep things lively and give you lots of directing options.

- Use the aisles as performance areas.
- Place a couple of stage flats at the end of each aisle, giving actors an off-stage area and a place to enter and exit. One of these areas will be the Bin.
- Create a varying range of rostra, or elevated platforms. The action can take place on and between these.

Design

This play comes alive in the moral choices that the characters face so avoid drawing the audience's focus from this. Keep your design choices simple and effective. I suggest that the stage flats start plain (or perhaps with some classic school signage – 'Reception' 'Staff room', etc.) and then get embellished. At each scene transition (and there are many), have a performer put up a poster on a flat, for example, 'No running', 'No chewing', 'No shouting'. By the end of the play there will be many of these. To create a sense of different, opposing camps, have a performer run on and spray graffiti over the posters, such as, 'Down with the Angels!', 'No Angels here!' or 'Angels out!', at the end of each act.

An opening suggestion

Play contemporary and upbeat music as the audience enter. The cast milling around, perhaps playing in a boisterous manner, with laughter and chat. When the audience are all in, create sudden and unexpected darkness, and sudden silence.

As the lights go down, think of using a single special projection:

> 'Quis Custodiet Ipsos Custodes?'
> 'Who Will Watch The Watchers?'
> Juvenal: Rome, 1st Century AD

After a few seconds of this we go straight into Jimmy's interrogation, and the play is underway with a sense of unease and disquiet.

Light

After the sinister opening scene, the play reverts to a very natural style. From that point it gradually gets darker and stranger. Allow the lights and sound to reflect this. A harsh spotlight on Jimmy as he sits, high and alone at the opening and close of the play will express something about the situation he is in. After this revert to a more naturalistic lighting state. As the play progresses, create atmosphere by occasionally introducing harsher and unusually-placed lamps. Floor lights will throw menacing shadows and coloured gels will add to the effect. Think of using a special spotlight and gobo to throw the shadow of prison bars on the stage-flats that represent the Rehabilitation Unit, or Bin.

Sound

Use sound to highlight the sense of paranoia that pervades this play. Think of having a low, sinister whisper in the short transitions between scenes. This can grow throughout the play and should be created by the actors. A dramatic sound of an echoing prison door swinging shut will add power to each moment a pupil gets 'binned'.

Costume

To root the play in the world of a single school, keep the costumes as naturalistic as possible. Don't worry about this making all the characters look the same: even a school uniform can articulate different pupils' characters. To help the audience swiftly differentiate among performers, use distinctive hairstyles, bags or spectacles for some key characters.

Transitions

Keep the transitions clean and efficient. Have your actors speak from the moment they can be seen. *Angels* has a momentum (more in ideas than in action) which your cast will need to pay attention to in order to wring the most meaning from the text.

A closing suggestion

Remember that the audience's theatrical experience doesn't end until they leave the venue. As the audience exits, think of playing music that reflects something of the disconcerting theme of the play – perhaps a slightly garbled and snarled medley of 'Suspicious Minds', 'Somebody's Watching Me' or 'Paranoia' would resonate.

The only way to approach *Angels* is as an ensemble piece where the responsibility for the play is shared across the cast. The suggestions above try to support this approach. Each actor should feel like they are performing from the moment the lights go down until the end of the play. If the cast invest their energy and enthusiasm as a team, they will be rewarded with audiences who are gripped by the tale and willing to engage in a debate that dates back far into human history. Each actor should ask themselves 'Could this happen?' and 'If it did, what would I do?'

For Caroline

Act One

Scene 1

Blackout.

A single spotlight is on Jimmy in his school uniform. He is wearing a fluorescent orange armband. He looks and sounds desperate and upset. He is talking to someone whose voice we hear but cannot see. It is a dark, disturbing, adult voice.

VOICE: Do you believe in Angels?

Pause. Jimmy is not sure what to say.

VOICE: *(Impatiently)* Do you believe in Angels?

JIMMY: I don't know.

VOICE: *(More impatiently)* Do you believe in Angels?

JIMMY: I don't know!   5

VOICE: Do you, Jimmy?

JIMMY: It wasn't just me! We were all going to do it and then … and then …

Pause.

VOICE: And then what?

JIMMY: *(Quietly)* And then it was just me.   10

VOICE: Are you saying that you did not know what you were doing? Are you saying that you have no mind of your own?

JIMMY: No! I'm just saying that it wasn't how it looked. I'm just saying that—   15

| VOICE: | You don't know what you're saying, do you? I'll tell you what you're saying, Jimmy. You are saying you have no faith in Angels. | |

VOICE: You don't know what you're saying, do you? I'll tell you what you're saying, Jimmy. You are saying you have no faith in Angels.

JIMMY: No, I—

VOICE: You have no faith in the system. 20

JIMMY: No, I—

VOICE: You are saying you want to bring the system down.

JIMMY: No, I'm just saying that I want … I want it to be like it used to be. 25

VOICE: Really? *(Pause)* Do you remember how it used to be? Before the Angels?

JIMMY: Yes.

VOICE: Do you? Do you really remember? I'm not sure you do. Let me remind you. Do you 30 remember an English lesson? About two weeks ago? Not so long ago, is it? You must remember.

The sounds of a classroom begin to grow in volume: students are talking and there are one or two occasional shouts.

JIMMY: I don't remember. I have a lot of English lessons. 35

VOICE: And they're all the same, are they?

JIMMY: I don't remember.

VOICE: Oh, I think you do, Jimmy. About two weeks ago you were late for an English lesson, Jimmy. Why was that? 40

Lights come up on a classroom full of students, some at their desks, some roaming and chatting.

JIMMY: I don't remember.

VOICE: I think you do. Why were you late, Jimmy?

JIMMY: I … I … don't remember …

SEAN: *(Off-stage, **taunting**)* Jimmy? Jimmy? Don't run
away from me, Jimmy! Come to Sean so   45
he can hurt you …

The spotlight on Jimmy blacks out.

Scene 2

A classroom.

*On the front row, Jess and Anika concentrate on a
lesson being delivered by an unseen teacher.
Beside them, Ollie is slumped head down on the
desk, using his folded arms as a pillow. Beside
him is an empty seat.*

*In the second row sit Harry and Hayley, drifting in
and out of concentration. There is an empty seat at
either end of this row.*

On the back row sit Kyle, Bradley, Jade and Beth.

SEAN: *(Off-stage, taunting)* Jimmy! Jimmy? Why are
you running, Jimmy? I only want to hurt you …

*Jimmy bursts into the classroom, quickly followed
by Sean and Aidan.*

*Aidan grabs hold of Jimmy from behind while Sean
thrusts his face threateningly into Jimmy's.*

SEAN: Gotcha, little piggy! And now I get to—

*Suddenly the whole class freezes and turns to face
the unseen teacher.*

The teacher is not heard by the audience; pauses indicate when she is speaking.

Sean and Aidan slowly release Jimmy without taking their eyes off the teacher.

SEAN: Yes, Miss, I know. We didn't hear the bell. *(Pause)* Yes, Miss, I know you're trying to   5
teach a lesson. We're sorry. Aren't we, Jimmy?

Sean slyly elbows Jimmy painfully in the ribs, then turns to the teacher and listens.

Pause.

SEAN: Sorry Miss, no Miss, it was an accident.

Jimmy goes to his seat at the front of the class, beside Jess, Anika and Ollie.

OLLIE: *(To Jimmy)* You alright?

Sean and Aidan snigger and wander off to their seats, pausing on their way to knock a pencil case and exercise book onto the floor, flirt with Beth and Jade, bend Bradley's fingers back till he yells and eventually sit and put their feet up on their desks, which are at opposite sides of the classroom.

As Sean and Aidan make their way, the rest of the class drift back into quiet chatter, ignoring the teacher. One or two concentrate occasionally.

OLLIE: What happened?

JIMMY: Nothing.   10

BETH: Miss, you got a pen I can borrow? *(Pause)* No, I know we're not writing at the moment. I'm not stupid, Miss, but I still need a pen.

(Pause) I'm writing something. *(Pause)* A
letter. *(Pause)* From a soldier in the war to   15
his mum. *(Pause)* The First World War, Miss.
(Pause) For history homework, Miss. *(She
pauses again, growing **indignant**)* But I've got
to do it by next lesson, Miss. Sir'll kill me.
(Pause) Thanks, Miss.   20

*Beth makes her way across the classroom, helps
herself to a pen from a pot to the side of the
classroom and heads back to her seat.*

BETH: Yeah, 'course I'll be quiet. I'm writing my letter.

She sits and starts writing.

BETH: *(Reading aloud as she writes)* Deeeeeear …
Muuumm …

She pauses and looks up.

BETH: Sorry, Miss.

She continues silently.

*Aidan and Sean start shouting to each other
across the classroom.*

SEAN: Oi! Aid!   25

AIDAN: What?

SEAN: Quack!

AIDAN: What d'you mean, quack? *(He turns to the
teacher and pauses to listen)* I dunno, Miss. He
just started quacking at me.   30

BETH: Miss, how d'you spell '**amputation**'?

*She pauses as the teacher begins to spell out the
word and then slowly writes it down.*

BETH:	A – m – p ... hang on! Hang on! Slow down!
AIDAN:	Oi! Sean!
SEAN:	What?
AIDAN:	Mooooo! 35
BRADLEY:	*(Grinning)* Miss, I'm concerned that my fellow students are disrupting my education. And I think my friend Kyle feels the same way. Don't you, Kyle?
KYLE:	*(Grinning)* Yes, Miss, I find it very, very 40 disappointing.
BRADLEY:	You see, Miss, *Macbeth* is a very challenging – fascinating, yes, but challenging – play and I don't think the attitude of some students in the class is helping my learning. 45 D'you think we could just give up and play Hangman?
SEAN:	Aid!
AIDAN:	Yeah?
SEAN:	Cockadoodledoo! 50
HAYLEY:	*(Standing and speaking furiously to Sean)* Oh, for goodness' sake, can't you be quiet? Can't you just shut up and do what you're told?
AIDAN AND SEAN:	*(Mocking)* Oooooooh!
SEAN:	Miss, it's a mouse *(he points at Hayley)* 55 and it roars like a lion!

Jade snatches Beth's pen.

BETH:	Aagh! Give it back, you slapper!

Jade snaps Beth's pen.

BETH: Miss, Jade's broke your pen, Miss.

ANIKA: *(To Jess)* Oh, this is pointless. I've got no idea
what she's talking about cos I can't hear. 60
They're making farm noises. No one's
listening. Why does she keep talking when
no one's listening, no one cares and no one
can hear her even if they did care?

*Aidan starts tearing pages out of his exercise
book, crumpling them into balls and throwing
them at Sean.*

JESS: What do you think of that Angels thing 65
Mr Stone was on about this morning?

ANIKA: He asked me if I wanted to be one – to be an
Angel.

JESS: Me too. You gonna do it?

ANIKA: Dunno. What do you reckon? 70

JIMMY: What do you have to do?

JESS: Don't you ever listen in assembly?

JIMMY: Er …

ANIKA: It's like being a prefect. You just keep your
eyes open and if you see someone 75
misbehaving or being anti-social, you let
Mr Stone know.

JIMMY: And what does Mr Stone do about it?

OLLIE: Kills them. Slowly. Talks them to death.

ANIKA: Depends what they've done. They've got 80
this new isolation place. Like a sin bin.
They're gonna stick naughty kids in there for
a day or two.

| JIMMY: | Like that'll make a difference. Just keeps them out the way for a bit. | 85 |

JIMMY: Like that'll make a difference. Just keeps them out the way for a bit. 85

JESS: What about you, Ollie?

OLLIE: What about what?

JESS: Are you going to be an Angel?

OLLIE: Naah. Can't be bothered. They haven't asked me, anyway. 90

JIMMY: Sounds like the quickest way to get your head kicked in.

As Aidan throws more paper at him, Sean loses his temper.

SEAN: You do that one more time and I'll kill you. I mean it.

AIDAN: No you don't. 95

SEAN: I'm warning you, Aid.

JESS: I'm gonna do it. I mean – look at this lot. Something needs to happen. *(Nodding in the direction of the teacher)* She's not going to do anything about it, is she? 100

JIMMY: *(Looking at the teacher)* Why is she so sweaty?

OLLIE: Fear.

JIMMY: Fear? What of?

OLLIE: Us.

JIMMY: What do you mean, 'us'? It's *them* she 105
should be scared of. *(He nods at Sean)* He burnt down the science block, for God's sake.

JESS: Everyone *says* he burnt down the science block.

JIMMY:	Everyone *knows* he burnt down the science block.	110
JESS:	Go on, Anika. I'll do it if you will.	
ANIKA:	Do what?	
JESS:	Be an Angel.	
ANIKA:	I dunno.	115
JIMMY:	It's not going to make any difference. You'll just get picked on by the—	

Everyone in the classroom freezes and looks in surprise at the teacher. Jimmy has been caught talking when he should have been listening. As Jimmy speaks to the teacher, Aidan and Sean begin to chant his name quietly, growing louder.

JIMMY:	I don't know, Miss.	
AIDAN AND SEAN:	Jim-my, Jim-my, Jim-my …	
JIMMY:	I *was* listening, Miss.	120
AIDAN AND SEAN:	Jim-my, Jim-my, Jim-my …	
JIMMY:	I was listening but I don't know the answer, Miss. Sorry, Miss.	
AIDAN AND SEAN:	Jim-my, Jim-my, Jim—	

Aidan and Sean suddenly stop. The teacher has had enough and is telling Sean off. Furious, he argues back while Aidan laughs.

| SEAN: | You always pick on me. Never anyone else. You hate me, don't you? What about him? *(He indicates Aidan)* Are you sending him out? No, didn't think so. | 125 |

Pause.

SEAN: *(Standing)* Alright, I'm going, I'm going. Better
        out than in. *(He smiles and makes his way*   130
        casually to the classroom door) Enjoy the rest
        of the lesson, everyone! Pay attention. Don't
        be naughty. Work hard. Listen to the nice
        teacher. Write down everything she says. *(He*
        reaches the classroom door and then turns to the
        class) Don't worry about me, I'll be fine.   135
        I'll go and have a nice little chat with
        Mr Stone while you lot sit here and—

        *Sean stops suddenly, **flinching** as though the*
        teacher is bellowing at him.

SEAN: *(Bellowing back)* I SAID I'M GOING AND I
        AM. OK?

        Sean leaves and slams the door behind him.

        Blackout.

Scene 3

Breaktime a couple of days later.

Beth and Jade are to one side, talking, laughing
*and **bickering**. Beth is eating a bag of crisps; Jade*
is eating an apple.

Jimmy, Ollie and Anika are talking.

*Enter Jess. She is wearing a **fluorescent** orange*
armband. Jimmy stares and laughs.

JIMMY: What is *that*?

JESS: What is what?

JIMMY: You look like a lollipop lady!

| JESS: | Without the lollipop. Or the high-visibility coat. Or the miserable face. But, yeah, other than that, I look *just* like a lollipop lady. | 5 |

JIMMY: What is it?

JESS: It's my Angels armband.

JIMMY: What do you mean? 10

JESS: It means I'm an Angel.

ANIKA: *(Hugging her)* You've always been an Angel to me, mate.

Ollie mimes sticking two fingers down his throat.

JIMMY: Don't you feel a bit … you know … a bit …

JESS: Stylish? Glamorous? 15

JIMMY: No, I mean don't you feel a bit …

OLLIE: Of a prat?

JIMMY: No, I mean a bit … **vulnerable**?

JESS: No. Why would I? I mean, do you think I should? What do you mean? 20

JIMMY: I dunno. It just makes you a bit of a …

OLLIE: Prat?

JIMMY: No, a bit of a … target. Doesn't it?

JESS: A target for what?

JIMMY: Never mind. 25

ANIKA: I think it looks alright. Makes you look kind of important.

OLLIE: An important prat.

JESS: Oi, mind your language, potty mouth! You know what happens if I report you, don't you? 30

OLLIE:	I have to wash my potty mouth out with soap?
JESS:	You get sent to the Bin.
OLLIE:	*(In disbelief)* What?
JESS:	That's how it works. I report someone and they're off – into the Bin. That's what they call it. The Sin Bin. It's actually called the Rehabilitation Unit but everyone's calling it the Bin.
OLLIE:	When did all this start?
JESS:	Yesterday.
ANIKA:	Did you hear about that kid in the year below? Little ginger kid. What's his name?
JIMMY:	Is he called Belly?
ANIKA:	I don't think that's what his mum calls him but, yeah, that's him.
JIMMY:	*(Gangsta voice)* He's a right gangsta.
ANIKA:	Yeah. Anyway, he got put in the Bin yesterday morning. Swore at a teacher. Got two days.
JIMMY:	Good. He's a nasty little …
ANIKA:	But when he was in there, he went mental. Kicking and screaming and everything. His mum had to come and pick him up. I saw her taking him home. Now she won't let him come to school. She says what they're doing in there is illegal.
JIMMY:	What the hell *are* they doing in there?
ANIKA:	Dunno. But if Belly couldn't take it, it must be pretty bad. He's had a detention every lunchtime since September. He told me he

35

40

45

50

55

60

likes them cos it's nice and warm and he gets
to hang around with all his mates. So he
loves detentions … but he cries like a baby
when he has to go in the Bin. Makes you   65
wonder, doesn't it?

*Still at a distance, Jade and Beth are taking an
interest in Jess's armband, pointing and laughing.*

OLLIE: Did you know, the Nazis used to make
people stick their hands in boiling water.
And then they pulled their teeth out.

JIMMY: Why?   70

OLLIE: I dunno. For fun, maybe?

JIMMY: Oi, Anika. You know you saw Belly going
home?

ANIKA: Yeah?

JIMMY: Did he have all his teeth? Any missing? 75

ANIKA: Dunno. Didn't count his teeth. Couldn't get
close enough.

JIMMY: Any bandages on his hands?

ANIKA: Don't think so …

JIMMY: Probably not doing the Nazi torture then, 80
Ollie.

OLLIE: Not yet, Jimmy. Not yet …

Jade and Beth approach.

BETH: *(Pointing to Jess's armband)* What's that?

JESS: It's my arm. I've got another one on the
other side.   85

BETH: Very funny. Like me to break your arm? Tell
us another joke like that and I might just do it.

13

JADE: *(Barging Jess)* Think you look good in it? Think you're something special?

ANIKA: Give it a rest, girls.   90

JIMMY: You could report them for that, Jess. You could get them put in the Bin.

JESS: Shut up, Jimmy.

BETH: Don't think orange is your colour, love.

JADE: Don't think armbands are gonna be big on   95
the catwalk this year.

ANIKA: Is that *don't* think? Or *can't* think?

BETH: What's that? What did you say?

JIMMY: Go on, Jess. Report them. *(To Beth and Jade)*
She's an Angel, so you'd better watch what   100
you say.

JADE: *(Laughs)* Oooh! She's an Angel! She's an
Angel and she's going to report us.

BETH: *(Laughs)* Where's your wings, love? Don't
look much like an angel.   105

JIMMY: Go on, Jess.

*Enter Sean and Aidan, chatting, laughing and
sparring.*

BETH: Yeah, go on, Jess. Report us. Go on. Think
I'm scared of that Bin? Think I'm scared of
you? Think I'm scared of a fat ugly bird with
bad hair and an orange armband? Don't   110
think so.

SEAN: Whoa, whoa, whoa, what's going on here
then? Bit of a do? Bit of trouble? *(To Beth and
Jade)* Is this man bothering you, ladies?

JADE: His face is bothering me.   115

SEAN: *(To Jimmy)* You heard the lady. Your face is bothering her. Turn round and stop upsetting her with your ugly face.

Jimmy looks pleadingly to Jess for help. She is staring firmly at her feet. Sean steps threateningly closer to Jimmy.

SEAN: *(Slowly and threateningly)* I said turn around and stop upsetting her with your nasty,   120 ugly face.

Jimmy gives in and turns around.

AIDAN: The back's not much better than the front.

SEAN: It's the smell. That's the problem, I reckon. Get a bit further away, Jimmy. Go on.

Sean pushes Jimmy away, his back still turned to them. Sean sniffs.

SEAN: Bit further.   125

Jimmy takes another step or two. Sean sniffs again.

SEAN: Bit further.

Jimmy takes another step. Sean sniffs.

SEAN: And again.

Jimmy takes another step. Sean sniffs.

SEAN: That's better.

Laughing, Sean, Aidan, Beth and Jade wander off. Jess, Anika and Ollie are left avoiding each other's eyes. Jimmy turns back around.

JIMMY: You didn't do anything. You just stood there. What's the point of being an Angel if you're just going to stand there? 130

Pause.

JIMMY: *(Angrily)* You're *supposed* to make a difference.

Blackout.

Scene 4

Breaktime the following day.

A bell rings. Enter Beth and Jade who wander to their usual breaktime place and start eating.

Enter Hayley and Harry, wearing orange armbands.

Enter Jess, Anika and Ollie, talking. Jess is wearing her orange armband.

JESS: *(Anxiously)* Shall we … er … not hang around here? *(More brightly)* Hey, does anyone want to go and get some food?

OLLIE: Can't be bothered.

ANIKA: *(To Jess)* What's the problem? 5

Anika notices Jade and Beth smiling forcedly at them.

ANIKA: It's not us that should be somewhere else. It's them. If you'd—

JESS: I know, I know, if I'd reported them then everything would be fine. The world would be a happy, happy place. It's just not that 10 easy …

ANIKA:	You still glad you did it?
JESS:	Did what?

She pokes Jess's orange armband.

ANIKA: This.

JESS: I think so. But it's difficult, you know. *(She   15
indicates Jade and Beth)* Like yesterday when
King Kong and her ugly sister were having a
go. You want to stop them but … it's
difficult. You thought any more about it?

ANIKA: Yeah.   20

JESS: Gonna do it?

ANIKA: Dunno. Maybe.

OLLIE: You're well out of it, I reckon.

ANIKA: *You're* well out of everything, I reckon. Do
nothing. Say nothing. Be nothing. Just …   25
breathe.

OLLIE: And sleep.

ANIKA: Sleep a lot.

OLLIE: Yeah, but it's not our job, is it? To watch over
those idiots, I mean. We're not the   30
zookeepers. We're just the monkeys in the
cages. And if zookeepers are a bit busy, they
don't get the monkeys to keep an eye on the
lions. Oi, you monkeys! Put on these orange
armbands and keep an eye on those   35
lions, would you? And watch out for those
tigers – they could turn ugly at any minute.
Let us know if they start savaging a koala,
would you?

| ANIKA: | What are you talking about? | 40 |

OLLIE: God knows …

Enter Jimmy, wearing an orange armband.

OLLIE: You know you've got one of those armbands on, don't you?

JIMMY: Yeah! Mr Stone asked me to be an Angel. Good, eh? 45

OLLIE: *(Sarcastically)* Unbelievably fantastic. *(To himself)* Another one of the monkeys keeping an eye on things …

ANIKA: He asked *you* to be an Angel? *(She laughs)* They're not fussy then, are they? They'll 50 have any old rubbish … I'm not sure I want to join up now.

JIMMY: *(Flatly)* Ha, ha, very funny. Jess might have to report you for splitting my sides. *(Pause)* Or maybe she'll just leave me with my guts 55 hanging out of my sides, bleeding to death on the floor.

JESS: That isn't fair! I didn't—

JIMMY: Do a thing. Just stood there with your armband on and didn't do a thing. Stood 60 there while Sean Sutton and Aidan Woodward made me look an idiot and you didn't do a thing. I was getting totally humiliated and you didn't do a thing. Did you? No. So I'm going to show them. 65

ANIKA: Show them?

JIMMY: Yeah. Show them. Show them they can't—

*Enter Sean and Aidan. The moment they see Jimmy, they start to mock him **relentlessly**.*

SEAN: Look at him!

AIDAN: Look at him!

SEAN: *(Stroking his armband)* Don't you look smart. 70

AIDAN: *(Stroking his face)* Don't you look handsome in your little orange armband.

SEAN: Now you won't have to ask your little friend to get us sent to the Bin and be all sad when she's too chicken to do it. You can be too 75 scared to do it yourself. That's handy, isn't it?

JIMMY: Oh, you think I'm scared of you, do you?

AIDAN: Er … yeah.

JIMMY: Well, let me explain. See this?

Jimmy pulls a mobile phone from his pocket.

SEAN: Oh, yeah, I've seen one of them before. 80 That's what phones used to look like about thirty years ago, isn't it?

JIMMY: It might be a bit old but—

AIDAN: A bit? A bit? That's like saying my nan's a bit old.

JIMMY: All I have to do is send a text and you get 85 sent to the Bin. See?

SEAN: Send a text? Who to?

JIMMY: I dunno. All I have to do is send the right message from the right phone and if your name's in the text, you're off to the Bin. See? 90

SEAN: Serious?

JIMMY: Serious.

AIDAN: Hang on, hang on. What do you mean the right message from the right phone?

JIMMY: The text has to be sent from an Angel's   95
phone and it has to have a codeword in it.

SEAN: What's the codeword?

JIMMY: Changes every day.

SEAN: So what is it today?

JIMMY: I'm not telling you that! And if you get   100
caught messing with an Angel's phone then
that's a week in the Bin, no questions,
straight. So who's scared now?

Pause. Aidan thinks.

AIDAN: Give me that phone.

JIMMY: No.   105

AIDAN: Go on, give me the phone. I just want to
have a look at it.

JIMMY: I can't show you the phone cos I've already
put the codeword in a text. And your names.
Just in case.   110

SEAN: You've *what*?

JIMMY: You heard. I've got a text ready to go. I just
press 'Send' and you're off to the Bin.

AIDAN: But we haven't done anything.

JIMMY: And that's why I haven't sent it yet. But you   115
annoy me and I'll send it. I mean it.

SEAN: Annoy you? Us?

AIDAN: Go on, let's have a look at your phone. Your
lovely phone. Can you really send texts from

something that old? Do you put LOL in it?   120
Do you—

JIMMY: *(Brandishing the phone)* I'm warning you.

SEAN: He's bluffing. There's no codeword. He
hasn't got anything to text and he's got no
one to text it to.   125

JIMMY: Whatever you say, Sean.

Aidan is getting more aggressive and threatening.
He tries to grab the phone.

AIDAN: Go on, show us your phone. Go on.

JIMMY: I'm warning you. You stop it now.

SEAN: Go on, Jimmy boy. Show him your phone.
Show him your secret spy codeword. Show   130
him your Mission Impossible secret message.

Sean and Aidan are now pushing Jimmy from one
to the other and back.

AIDAN: You can't do it, can you? You can't do it.
You're too scared. Like your little friend.

SEAN: *(Looking around for Jess)* Where's she gone?
Run away cos the bad boys are here?   135

AIDAN: Go on, then, press it, press 'Send'. Send it
now, you little—

*Jimmy presses 'Send'. All freeze in **anticipation**.*
Nothing happens. Slowly Aidan and Sean realise
that nothing has happened. They start to laugh.

SEAN: What an idiot! What a—

He is interrupted by a mechanical buzz from
loudspeakers in the corridor. A prerecorded

message plays, with the students' names inserted in a different voice.

VOICE 1: Attention. This is a disciplinary announcement. Attention. This is a disciplinary announcement. Would … 140

VOICE 2: … Sean Sutton and Aidan Woodward …

VOICE 1: … please make your way to the Rehabilitation Unit.

Sean and Aidan look up, spin around and stare open-mouthed in disbelief.

OLLIE: *(To himself)* Monkeys two, lions nil. 145

SEAN: What?

VOICE 2: Sean Sutton and Aidan Woodward.

VOICE 1: You have two minutes to make your way to the Rehabilitation Unit.

AIDAN: This is taking the pi— 150

VOICE 2: Sean Sutton and Aidan Woodward.

VOICE 1: You have been placed in the Rehabilitation Unit for one day. Failure to attend promptly will result in your placement being extended. You have less than two minutes to report 155 to the Rehabilitation Unit.

JIMMY: *(Enjoying himself enormously)* What were you saying a minute ago, Sean? Something about me being an idiot?

SEAN: Is this a joke? 160

AIDAN: Turn it off, eh, Jimmy? Tell them you made a mistake and we'll have a talk about it, eh?

JIMMY: Was it a minute ago? Maybe, I don't know. Time goes so fast when you're enjoying yourself, doesn't it? 165

SEAN: *(Limbering up to fight)* This is gonna hurt you more than it hurts me, Jimmy.

VOICE 2: Sean Sutton and Aidan Woodward.

VOICE 1: You have one minute to report to the Rehabilitation Unit. 170

JIMMY: *(Grinning)* See? Told you it was a minute ago.

AIDAN: We'd better go, Sean.

SEAN: Shut up, Aid. You think I'm getting in trouble cos of him? Cos he's sent some poxy text? I'm not going nowhere till I've kicked his— 175

JIMMY: Not my fault, Sean. I'm an Angel. And that's what Angels do. They keep things how they should be. They keep people like you out of trouble.

VOICE 2: Sean Sutton and Aidan Woodward. 180

VOICE 1: You have thirty seconds to report to the Rehabilitation Unit.

SEAN: *(Shouting at the voices)* That wasn't thirty seconds! You said it was a minute and then you said it was thirty seconds and it never 185 was! You're going too fast. You can't count! That isn't fair!

AIDAN: *(Trying to drag him away)* Sean, come on. We've gotta go.

SEAN: *(At the voices)* Come and make me! You 190 want me? Come and get me!

AIDAN: Sean! Sean! I'm going. You coming?

SEAN: *(At the voices)* Come on! Come and get me!

Ignored, Aidan gives up and runs.

VOICE 2:   Sean Sutton and Aidan Woodward.

VOICE 1:   You have failed to attend the   195
          Rehabilitation Unit within two minutes. As a
          result your placement has been extended to
          two days.

*Jimmy and the others back away from Sean. The
lights fade as Sean rants increasingly furiously
until he is left in a spotlight, facing the audience.*

SEAN: *(At the voices)* You're joking me!

VOICE 1:   Failure to attend in one minute from   200
          now will result in your placement being
          extended by a further day.

SEAN: You can't do this. Do you hear me? You can't
          do this. Jimmy? Jimmy? You're gonna be
          sorry. You're gonna be *so* sorry.   205

VOICE 2:   Sean Sutton.

VOICE 1:   You have thirty seconds remaining in which
          to report to the Rehabilitation Unit.

SEAN: It's not fair! It's not fair! You're gonna wish
          you'd never been born, Jimmy. You're   210
          gonna wish it was you, not me. Not me!
          Not me!

Blackout.

Act Two

Scene 1

Breaktime two weeks later.

A bell rings. Enter Hayley and Harry, wearing their orange armbands. They pause and chat silently in a corner.

Enter Jimmy, Ollie, Anika and Jess, chatting. Jimmy and Jess are still wearing their orange armbands.

ANIKA: I'm just saying I haven't had a laugh in a lesson for two weeks. I'm just saying it used to be fun sometimes.

JIMMY: No, you're saying it used to be better before the Angels. 5

ANIKA: I'm just saying that sometimes – not all the time, just sometimes – when Sean and Aidan and the others were messing about in lessons, sometimes – not all the time – *sometimes* it was quite funny. 10

JIMMY: Like when, for example?

ANIKA: I dunno. Like …

JIMMY: Like when Sean Sutton pinned me down in history and wrote on my face?

ANIKA: No, but … 15

JIMMY: Like when Sean Sutton set fire to my pencil case in science?

ANIKA: No.

JIMMY: Like when Sean Sutton and Aidan Woodward

told everyone they saw me in the mini-
market wearing my mum's clothes? 20

ANIKA: No, that wasn't funny, it was horrible.

JIMMY: When then?

ANIKA: Like when Aidan shut Mr Nolan in the
cupboard at the back of his room. That was 25
funny.

JIMMY: And you think Mr Nolan agrees with you?
I don't remember him looking too smiley
when they let him out. I don't remember him
having a good old laugh and slapping Aidan 30
on the back and sharing the moment with
his old buddy Aidan. Do you?

ANIKA: No, he got him suspended.

JIMMY: So that's my point. Why is it not funny to be
horrible to me and funny to be horrible to 35
Mr Nolan? What's the difference?

ANIKA: Cos … cos … all I'm saying is we don't have
a laugh in lessons any more. Everyone just
sits there doing what they're told. Not cos
they want to, not cos they're listening, not 40
cos they want to learn. It's cos they're *scared*.

JIMMY: But if they're doing what they're told, there's
nothing to be scared of. That's why the
Angels thing is so good. Isn't it, Jess?

JESS: I dunno. 45

JIMMY: Come on! You're an Angel, you must think
it's a good thing.

JESS: Must I? How many people have you reported
then, Jimmy? How many people have you put
in the Bin? 50

JIMMY:	I dunno. Five or six, maybe?
JESS:	It's eighteen, Jimmy. I've seen the league table on the notice board. It's eighteen and you know it is. You've only been an Angel for a couple of weeks, Jimmy. You're binning two people a day.

55

OLLIE: *(To himself)* Filthy habit.

JIMMY: So that's two people every day who get what they deserve. Two people who wouldn't get what they deserve if I didn't report them. Cos no teachers saw them. It was just me.

60

OLLIE: What about you, Jess? How many people have you reported?

JESS: None.

JIMMY: None?

65

JESS: None.

JIMMY: None? What do you mean, none?

JESS: It's like one – but one less. One take away one. Equals none – no one.

JIMMY: Why?

70

JESS: Maybe I don't see people being naughty. Maybe they see me and they stop. Maybe I don't like it. Maybe I wish I'd never said I'd be an Angel. I dunno.

ANIKA: Maybe she doesn't want to run round like Batman in full swing, punishing the bad guys and saving the world from the forces of evil.

75

JIMMY: It's a good thing to do. It's the *right* thing to do.

OLLIE: I got put in isolation once. Before they called it the Bin and all this Angels stuff started.

80

27

ANIKA: *(Amazed)* What? You?

OLLIE: Yeah, me. I used to be dangerous. I used to be a rebel. Hard man.

ANIKA: What did you do?

OLLIE: I talk in my sleep sometimes, you know – 85
when I'm dreaming. So I was having a sleep in Miss Long's English lesson in Year 7. And I had this dream I was arguing with my little brother. And I started swearing. Next thing I know, Miss Long's shouting at me. She 90
thought I was swearing at her.

JIMMY: I remember that! *(He laughs)* That was funny!

OLLIE: My mum didn't really get the joke. She grounded me for a week. Told me it was the most pathetic excuse she'd ever heard. And 95
she's heard a lot of my pathetic excuses …

ANIKA: See what I mean? That wouldn't happen now. Ollie doesn't sleep in lessons any more, do you?

OLLIE: Well … kind of. I've just started doing it with my eyes open. 100

*Enter Sean and Aidan. They are wearing
fluorescent orange t-shirts and seem wary and
embarrassed, almost crushed.*

JESS: I don't like that much, either.

OLLIE: What?

JESS: When they let you out of the Bin, you have to wear one of those t-shirts for a couple of weeks. Mr Stone says wearing school 105
uniform is a privilege and people who let the

school community down don't deserve to
wear it. So they make them wear those. It
shows you've been in the Bin. It means
you're a Binner.   110

OLLIE: God, when I was in isolation they just sat you
in a room with that old lady for a day. They
didn't give you a leaving present – and make
you wear it for a week.

JESS: The good old days, eh?   115

JIMMY: *(Arrogantly, to Sean and Aidan)* Here come the
Binners! Alright boys? Looking good! Being
good?

ANIKA: *(Amazed, whispering)* Jimmy, what are you
doing?   120

*Sean steps aggressively towards Jimmy. Aidan
pulls Sean away.*

AIDAN: *(Anxiously)* Alright, Jimmy?

Sean and Aidan talk quietly in a corner.

JESS: What's happened to those two? A couple of
weeks ago they'd have danced on his face for
saying that.

ANIKA: It must be the Bin.   125

JIMMY: Of course it's the Bin. It changes people. It
makes them good.

OLLIE: What do they do to them in there? It's like …
magic or something.

JIMMY: Who cares, if it works?   130

Blackout.

Scene 2

Breaktime a couple of days later.

A bell rings. Enter Bradley and Kyle, wandering about.

Enter Jimmy, Hayley and Harry from the opposite direction; all are wearing their orange armbands.

JIMMY: I just looked at him. I swear. I gave him one look and he stopped.

HARRY: So what did you do?

JIMMY: Reported him, of course.

HAYLEY: How many's that now?   5

JIMMY: *(Proudly)* Twenty-three.

HARRY: But he stopped hitting the other kid, didn't he?

HAYLEY: But would he have stopped if you hadn't turned up? *(Pause)* 'Course he wouldn't.

JIMMY: Exactly.   10

HAYLEY: That's the power of the Angels. See, Harry? They're frightened of us – frightened of what we can do.

HARRY: They're not frightened of us, they're frightened of getting binned.   15

HAYLEY: Same thing.

Jimmy, Hayley and Harry walk towards, and pass, Bradley and Kyle.

BRADLEY: Don't shoot! Don't shoot!

KYLE: We'll be good, I promise!

Exit Bradley and Kyle, laughing.

Enter Jess, Anika and Ollie.

JIMMY: Hey, Jess! We're going up to the Angels' common room at lunch-time. They're 20
doing free cakes and stuff. You coming?

JESS: No, I ... er ... I've got some ... er ... stuff. Stuff I need to do.

JIMMY: Okay.

JESS: Maybe, er ... maybe see you up there 25
tomorrow.

But Jimmy, Hayley and Harry are talking among themselves, not listening.

ANIKA: Doesn't want to talk to us any more, does he?

OLLIE: Who?

ANIKA: Jimmy! Who did you think I meant?

OLLIE: Oh, yeah, Jimmy. Right. What's he on about, 30
free cakes and stuff?

JESS: In the Angels' common room. The old D and T room, they've turned it into a common room. Comfy chairs, vending machines, carpet. Someone said they're going to put a telly in 35
there. It's a special place for special people.

ANIKA: How come you're not in there?

JESS: Same reason I don't sit on the Angels' tables in the canteen. Rather hang around with you lot, I suppose. God knows why ... 40

They laugh.

OLLIE: It's a privileged life in the Angels, isn't it? Free cakes, carpet, your own table for dinner ... I might join up.

JESS: Don't. All they talk about is who they've reported, who did what to who, who 45 reported them, who's got the most reports. You know they've got a league table, don't you? You get a point every time you report someone and get them binned.

OLLIE: Ooh, exciting. Where are you in the league, 50 Jess?

JESS: Relegation zone, I reckon. You know what happens if you're in the top ten at the end of the year? A week in Florida, that's what I heard.

ANIKA: No! You joking? Who pays? 55

JESS: They do.

OLLIE: No! That'd cost *(he starts mental calculations)* ten plane tickets, ten hotel rooms ... that's ... a lot of money.

ANIKA: Thousands. 60

JESS: That's what I heard.

OLLIE: Well, don't just stand here talking to us. Get out there and arrest someone!

JESS: Yeah, right.

OLLIE: Can you take a friend to Florida if you win? 65 I've always loved you, Jess ...

JESS: Don't pack your suitcase just yet.

ANIKA: Still not binned anyone?

JESS: Nah. I mean, if I saw someone getting murdered I would. 70

OLLIE: What – even if it was me?

JESS: Maybe. *(Pause)* It's just ... I dunno. You see some kid dropping litter or ... saying

something nasty … or whatever … and you
don't wanna get involved. You don't want   75
them to do it but you don't want to be the
one to stop them. D'you know what I mean?

OLLIE: Yeah, but think about Florida. Sun, sand,
DisneyWorld! You're not gonna be getting a
hug off Mickey Mouse talking like that, are   80
you?

*While Jess, Anika and Ollie are still talking,
attention shifts to Harry, Hayley and Jimmy.*

JIMMY: What I don't get is this. If the ten best Angels
go to Florida, who's gonna look after things
here? I mean, it could all fall apart in a week,
couldn't it?   85

HAYLEY: I'm sure you'll manage without me, Jimmy.

JIMMY: Oh, you reckon you're going to Florida, do
you? And you reckon I'm not?

HAYLEY: 'Course. *(Proudly)* Mr Stone says I'm the
brightest of all the Angels!   90

HARRY: Did he say that? Dirty old man!

HAYLEY: Are you insulting a teacher, Harry? *(She gets
out her phone)* You know what that means,
don't you? Anyway, he's not a dirty old man.
He just knows quality when he sees it.   95

JIMMY: What does he mean, the brightest of all the
Angels? You don't have to be clever to be an
Angel. Do you?

HAYLEY: No, you just have to be good. And good at
making other people be good.   100

HARRY: And good at catching other people *not* being good.

HAYLEY: It's power, Jimmy. It's responsibility. You have to know how to use it. I mean, look at your little friend over there. What's her name? 105

JIMMY: Jess.

HAYLEY: Yeah, her. They gave her the armband and she doesn't know what to do with it. She's not an Angel. She's a girl with an armband. There's a difference. 110

Enter Jade and Beth, wearing orange Binner t-shirts.

Jimmy nudges Harry and Hayley who turn and look.

HAYLEY: Whoa! Look at this lot. You got binned! Who got you? What did you do this time?

JADE: *(Angrily)* You think cos you've got that thing on your arm we have to take your sh—

HAYLEY: Oi! Watch it! 115

BETH: Shut it, Jade. I'm not getting binned again. Not for you and your mouth, alright? Just keep moving.

JIMMY: *(To Jade)* Remember me? How does my face look now? 120

Jess, Anika and Ollie look shocked; Harry looks surprised; Hayley looks delighted.

JADE: Dunno what you're talking about.

BETH: *(Quietly grim)* Drop it, Jimmy.

JIMMY: Oh, you can remember a couple of days back, can't you? You've got enough brain left to remember that, haven't you? A few brain   125 cells to rub together?

Beth moves on. Jade opens her mouth to speak. Jimmy gets out his phone and holds it up to her.

JIMMY: Remember what you said to me, do you? This face still bothering you, is it?

Jimmy pushes his face into Jade's, brandishing his phone and writing a text.

JIMMY: Is it? Is it? Let me know and I can sort that out. I can sort it so you don't see this face   130 for a day or two – maybe longer. A couple of days back in the Bin – is that what you want? Is it? Is it?

HARRY: Alright, Jimmy. Calm down, mate.

JIMMY: *(Brandishing his phone)* All I have to do is   135 send this and you're back to the Bin. Cos that's where you two belong. In the Bin.

HARRY: Jimmy …

JIMMY: Got anything you want to say to me? Want to have a go? Eh? No?   140

*Pause. Jade **reluctantly** submits.*

JIMMY: *(Giving Jade a push)* So you just walk away nice and quietly like a good girl. OK? You keep your head down and your mouth shut and you walk away. OK?

BETH: *(Quietly)* Come on, Jade. Let's go.   145

Exit Jade and Beth. Jimmy visibly relaxes as they go. Harry looks surprised. Hayley looks impressed.

HAYLEY: Nice one, Jimmy.

JIMMY: I'm going to the common room. Coming?

Exit Jimmy, Hayley and Harry. Jess, Anika and Ollie watch them go, still open-mouthed at Jimmy's outburst.

Blackout.

Scene 3

Breaktime a couple of days later.

A bell rings. Jimmy, Harry, and Hayley are talking. A Year 7 boy hangs around near Hayley.

Shane, Ed and Nav talk some distance behind them.

HARRY: Are we going up to the Angels' common room? What are we waiting for?

JIMMY: Dunno.

HAYLEY: Won't be a minute. Amy's just getting me something.

HARRY: Who's Amy?

JIMMY: *(Pointing at the Year 7 boy)* And who's he?

HAYLEY: Him? He's my little mate, aren't you?

The boy nods nervously. Jimmy and Harry stare at him, mystified. He looks away.

Enter Amy carrying a sausage roll. She hands it to Hayley.

5

HAYLEY: Thanks, Amy. Hang on. There's no napkin.
          I told you to wrap one end in a napkin. And   10
          now it's had your spitty little fingers all over
          it. D'you think I want to eat that? *(Amy shakes
          her head)* No, I don't. So what do you need to
          do?

AMY: *(Very quietly)* Get you another one.   15

HAYLEY: Yeah. You do. *(To Harry and Jimmy)* Sorry,
          won't be a minute. *(To Amy)* You still seem
          to be here. Why aren't you a cloud of dust
          in the distance?

*Amy mumbles something **inaudible**.*

HAYLEY: What? Speak up, you little—   20

AMY: *(Just **audible**)* I haven't got any more money.

HAYLEY: Your problem, not mine. So now you need to
          find some money *and* get me a sausage roll.
          I'm starting to lose my temper. Are you
          trying to annoy me? D'you *want* to go to   25
          the Bin?

Amy shakes her head furiously.

HAYLEY: You have one minute.

Amy runs.

JIMMY: What's going on? Why have you got kids
          fetching sausage rolls for you?

HAYLEY: I like sausage rolls. They don't do them in   30
          the Angels' common room.

JIMMY: Why don't you just go and get one from the
          canteen?

HAYLEY:	The canteen? Are you joking? Angels don't go into the canteen any more. 35
JIMMY:	*(Uncertainly)* Some of us do …
HAYLEY:	Some of you might do – but this one doesn't.
JIMMY:	But we've got our own table in the canteen …
HAYLEY:	I know we have but why would I want to sit there looking at a load of Binners? Puts me 40 off my food.
HARRY:	Where are you getting these kids from?
HAYLEY:	My little helpers? Oh, just around. Here and there. You want something done?
HARRY:	Erm … *(he looks around and down at himself)* 45 he could do my maths homework for me.
HAYLEY:	*(To the boy)* You! Whatsyername. You heard him.

The boy approaches Harry and looks expectantly and nervously up at him.

As they talk, a play fight breaks out among Shane, Ed and Nav. After a few seconds the noise starts to be noticeable but the fight never becomes any more than 'play'.

Enter Anika, who stops and watches from a distance.

HARRY:	I was joking. I haven't got any maths homework. Have I? 50
JIMMY:	I dunno. Get him to check. Oi, kid. Go and find out if we've got maths homework.
HAYLEY:	But don't ask a teacher. Understand?

The boy nods and runs.

HAYLEY: Might not look so good if a teacher sees him doing little jobs for us, eh? *(She notices the 'fight' going on behind them)* Oi! You lot! Come here! 55

Shane, Ed and Nav freeze, turn and approach, obviously scared. All talk at once.

SHANE: We were only—

ED: Messing about. Weren't we?

NAV: We didn't mean it. 60

SHANE: No, we never meant it. Did we?

NAV: We were just messing about.

ED: Yeah, just messing.

*Hayley snaps her fingers and holds a finger to her lips in one **deft** movement. She gets out her phone. All three instantly fall silent.*

HAYLEY: *(Indicating Shane)* You.

SHANE: Me? 65

HAYLEY: Yeah, that's why I pointed at you. You trying to annoy me?

Shane shakes his head furiously.

HAYLEY: What's your name?

SHANE: Shane Woods.

HAYLEY: You're binned, Shane Woods. 70

SHANE: What for?

HAYLEY: Fighting.

SHANE: Fighting? But we—

Hayley snaps her fingers and holds a finger to her lips again.

Silence.

HAYLEY: You arguing, Shane Woods?

Shane shakes his head again.

HAYLEY: How long d'you want to go for? A day? Two   75
days? Longer?

More head shaking from Shane.

HAYLEY: Or maybe you'd rather make yourself useful,
Shane Woods?

Shane nods desperately.

HAYLEY: Now today's your lucky day. I've got all the
help I need, but see him? *(She points to Harry)*   80
You follow round after him and do what he
says. OK? Whatever he says, you do.
Understand?

Shane nods.

HARRY: *(Uncertainly)* Thanks, Hayley.

HAYLEY: No problem.   85

Hayley looks at Harry expectantly.

HARRY: *(To Shane)* Er … go and get me … a glass of
water.

*Shane looks to Hayley. She nods. Exit Shane,
running.*

HAYLEY: Harry, you're pathetic. *(To Ed)* You. Come
here. *(Ed approaches)* What's your name?

ED: Edward. Edward Mills. 90

HAYLEY: Look at you, Edward Edward Mills. *(She messes his hair up)* Look at the state of you. *(She wipes her hand on the ground and then on his face)* Your hair's a mess. *(She pulls a button off his shirt)* Your face is filthy and your buttons are undone. You're in a state, boy. 95 What are you?

ED: In a state, Miss.

HAYLEY: You're a nasty, dirty, violent kid, aren't you, Edward Edward Mills? What are you?

ED: A dirty … violent … 100

HAYLEY: Not what I said but close enough. So what do we do with people like you?

ED: Put them in the Bin.

HAYLEY: But we don't want to go in the Bin, do we, Edward Edward Mills? 105

Ed shakes his head.

HAYLEY: So we make ourselves useful. *(To Jimmy)* D'you want him, Jimmy?

JIMMY: Er …

HAYLEY: See him? *(She points to Jimmy)* Follow him round and do what he says, OK? 110

Ed nods reluctantly and looks at Jimmy. Jimmy looks at Hayley who looks expectantly back. Shane returns with a cup of water for Harry.

JIMMY: I, er … I … why are you looking at me like that?

ED: I'm not looking at anyone like anything.

JIMMY:	Yeah, you are.	
ED:	*(Shrugging)* Your problem.	115
JIMMY:	*(Looks down)* My shoelace is undone. Do it up.	

Ed hesitates. He looks at Jimmy's shoes.

ED:	No, it isn't.
JIMMY:	Well, it's come loose then. It needs tightening.
HAYLEY:	Don't let him talk to you like that! Bin him! 120
JIMMY:	*(To Ed)* Undo it and do it up again. OK?

Ed shakes his head.

HAYLEY:	Bin him, Jimmy. Bin him.
JIMMY:	I said, undo it and do it up again.

Ed shakes his head.

JIMMY: Your choice, kid. *(He gets out his phone and writes a quick text)* Last chance. 125

When Ed does not respond, Jimmy presses 'Send'.

Pause.

As before, a prerecorded message is played over the loudspeakers.

VOICE 1: Attention. This is a disciplinary announcement. Attention. This is a disciplinary announcement. Would …

VOICE 2: … Edward Mills …

VOICE 1: … please make your way to the Rehabilitation Unit. 130

ED: OK, OK, I'll do it.

Ed kneels to do up the shoelace.

HAYLEY: *(Smiling)* Too late, Edward Edward Mills.
What's done is done and can't be undone.

VOICE 2: Edward Mills. 135

VOICE 1: You have two minutes to make your way to
the Rehabilitation Unit.

HAYLEY: You had your chance and you made your
choice. Jump a bit quicker next time, eh?

*As the voices drone on, Shane and Nav grin, then
splutter but cannot stop themselves laughing.*

Exit Ed, angry and frustrated.

JIMMY: Oh, so you think that's funny, do you? 140

They try but Nav and Shane can't stop laughing.

JIMMY: Stop it.

They can't. Jimmy gets angry and starts texting.

JIMMY: *(To Nav)* What's your name?

Silence.

JIMMY: *(To Shane)* What's his name?

SHANE: Nav Sadiq.

NAV: Hey! 145

JIMMY: *(Texting)* Nav Sadiq … and Shane Woods …

Jimmy presses 'Send'.

VOICE 1: Attention. This is a disciplinary
announcement. Attention. This is a
disciplinary announcement. Would …

VOICE 2:	… Nav Sadiq and Shane Woods …	150
VOICE 1:	… please make your way to the Rehabilitation Unit.	
VOICE 2:	Nav Sadiq and Shane Woods.	
VOICE 1:	You have two minutes to make your way to the Rehabilitation Unit.	155

Jimmy's grin fades as Nav and Shane exit; the recorded voices cut off soon afterwards.

JIMMY:	*(In disgust)* Kids!
HAYLEY:	You can see it, can't you? You can see what they'd be like if there weren't any Angels. They'd be mental. Out of control. Off the rails.
HARRY:	Someone's gotta keep them in line. 160
JIMMY:	D'you know what? I never knew teachers had such a tough job till I became an Angel. But kids like that make you realise what it's like.
HARRY:	Mind you, a lot of teachers let kids get away with anything. 165
HAYLEY:	Mistake. Big mistake. Let them get away with it once and they'll just keep pushing and pushing and pushing. They're like dogs. They need training.

Enter Amy with a sausage roll, one end wrapped in a napkin. She hands it to Hayley, who takes it but does not acknowledge Amy.

HAYLEY:	And that's why this school was in the state 170 it was before we came along. They try, the teachers, but it's not enough. They need people like us.

*Exit Hayley and Harry – Amy and the Year 7 boy
follow at a respectful distance. Jimmy is about to
exit when …*

Scene 4

ANIKA:	Hey, Jimmy!
JIMMY:	I'm going up to the common room with—
ANIKA:	Come over here.
JIMMY:	*(Calling after Hayley and Harry)* I'll catch up with you in a minute, Harry! I'll catch …

5

*They haven't heard him; he gives up and goes
over to Anika.*

JIMMY:	What?
ANIKA:	You didn't see me.
JIMMY:	What?
ANIKA:	I was standing over there.
JIMMY:	And?
ANIKA:	And you didn't see me.
JIMMY:	And?
ANIKA:	Well, for one thing, you used to notice when your friends came and stood about two metres away from you.
JIMMY:	And?
ANIKA:	And for another thing, you used to talk to your friends – not just stand there shouting 'And?' at them.
JIMMY:	OK, I'm sorry.

10

15

20

ANIKA: For what?

JIMMY: For the one thing …

ANIKA: And?

JIMMY: And the other thing. Now you're doing it.

ANIKA: What?   25

JIMMY: *(Mimicking her)* And? And?

ANIKA: Sorry. And for a third thing, you used to be
           … nice … kind.

JIMMY: What do you mean?

ANIKA: Didn't you notice what you did to those kids 30
           a minute ago? You were there – you must
           have noticed. Or did you nip out for a minute?

JIMMY: I don't know what you mean.

ANIKA: Jimmy, you were treating them like *dirt*. At
           one point, Hayley was wiping a kid's face   35
           with dirt. What's happened to her? She used
           to be … alright.

JIMMY: You don't get it, do you?

ANIKA: No, I don't.

JIMMY: Those kids got what they deserved. You let 40
           them get away with it and they just keep
           pushing. D'you remember the state this
           school was in before the Angels came?

ANIKA: I remember what you used to be like – and
           you weren't getting kids to do up your   45
           shoelaces.

JIMMY: Listen. Those kids were fighting.

ANIKA: Hardly.

JIMMY: Those kids *were* fighting. And when kids

behave like that, when they're bad enough   50
to get sent to the Bin cos they're not fit to be
a part of the school community, they give up
any right to be treated like a decent member
of that community.

ANIKA: Who told you that? Did you read it   55
somewhere? Do they make you learn it off by
heart?

JIMMY: No! It's true. This school used to be hell.
Maybe not for you but it was for me. The
whole place was out of control. It was bad   60
enough in lessons but out here, it was …
dangerous. Even the teachers used to go
round in pairs cos they didn't want to be out
here on their own. Now it feels safe.

ANIKA: Safe? For who? *You* feel safe. *You* feel in   65
control. But what about everyone else?

JIMMY: The Angels keep it safe for everyone.

ANIKA: And who's keeping everyone safe from the
Angels? *(Pause)* I know Sean and that lot
used to give you a bit of a hard time—   70

JIMMY: A *bit* of a hard time?

ANIKA: But look at you now. You're doing what they
used to do to you. What's going on? What are
you after? Revenge?

JIMMY: *(Increasingly angry)* I'm just doing what an   75
Angel does. Holding things together.
Keeping things how they should be. Keeping
people how they ought to be. It isn't revenge.
It's justice. Look at us. Look at this place.
We're not one big happy family, we're not   80

all in it together. You need to control people who can't control themselves. And if they can't or they won't, if they decide they're not going to stick to the rules, then they have to accept the consequences. *They* decide what 85 happens to them – the way they act, the things they do. They decide. It's not me that makes them bad. It's them. Not me. It's them. Not me.

Exit Jimmy.

Blackout.

Act Three

Scene 1

After school a couple of days later.

Enter Jade wearing an orange Binner T-shirt. Enter Jess. They stand apart, avoiding eye contact.

JADE: You spying on me? Making sure I'm being good?

JESS: Eh? No. I'm on patrol. Have to stand here every Monday break, dinner time and after school. Fighting crime and beating the bad   5
guys. You spying on me?

JADE: No, I'm waiting for Beth. I just got out of the Bin. Said I'd meet her here.

JESS: Beth didn't get binned with you?

JADE: Nah. Beth's a good girl now. She says she's   10
never getting binned again.

JESS: But you and Beth were always … you know …

JADE: Partners in crime? Yeah, I know. But she knows when to shut up.

JESS: And you …   15

JADE: I know when I should have shut up and it's usually about ten minutes ago. So I got binned.

JESS: How many times have you been binned now?

JADE: Twice now. That's the last time, mind. I'm never getting binned again. You watch. I   20
swear I'm never going back there.

JESS: Bad, is it? *(Pause)* What actually … I mean, what happens in there? What do they do?

JADE: *(Cagily)* It's alright. It's nothing. *(Smiles)* It's a
          holiday camp. Sauna, hot tub, spa   25
          treatments, room service …

JESS: But you're never going back.

JADE: Nope.

JESS: So it works. Makes people behave.

JADE: *(Shrugging)* S'pose so. Like I said, I'm never   30
          going back.

          Pause.

JADE: It used to be fun, you know? It used to be a
          laugh. You mess about, you have a laugh, you
          get caught, you get done for it and it's all
          forgotten. That's how it used to be. But now   35
          there's no fun any more. No one wants a
          laugh nowadays. They're all too … scared.

JESS: What of?

JADE: The Bin. What else?

JESS: But what are they so scared of in the Bin?   40

JADE: *(Quietly)* They say you get a week in there if
          you talk about it.

          Pause.

JADE: *(Laughing)* It's a holiday camp.

          Pause.

JADE: *(Quietly)* You won't … you won't say anything,
          will you? About … what we talked about?   45

JESS: 'Course not.

          *They stand, avoiding eye contact again as though
          the exchange had never happened.*

          Blackout.

Scene 2

Jess and Jade still stand avoiding eye contact.

Enter Jimmy, Hayley and Harry.

HAYLEY: Alright, Jess?

JESS: *(Coldly)* Yup.

HAYLEY: Binned anyone today?

JESS: Nope.

HAYLEY: Binned anyone ever? *(She laughs)*   5

Enter Amy.

HAYLEY: Alright, girl? What's the news?

AMY: Stephen Cook said something about Josh
Brown's mum so Josh smacked him.

HAYLEY: Is that it? *(She nods)* Good. Stay close, I might
need you to do something for me.   10

Enter Shane wearing an orange Binner t-shirt.

HARRY: Shane! How's things?

SHANE: Vicky Barratt sprayed deodorant in Tanya
Price's face … and … er … Nav says that
Lloyd heard that Jordan saw someone
kicking Sam Lowe.   15

HARRY: Someone?

SHANE: Yeah. Some kid.

HARRY: Bit short on detail, Shane. But … er … nice
try. Keep it up. But get better. OK?

SHANE: I'll try.   20

HAYLEY: Yeah, try harder.

Enter Ed, in an orange Binner t-shirt, running and panting.

JIMMY: Ed. Got anything for me?

ED: Sophie Gates fell down the stairs by the tech rooms. She's not moving. She's bleeding. She's— 25

JIMMY: Who pushed her?

ED: I dunno. No one.

JIMMY: So it was an accident?

ED: I dunno. She screamed and she fell. She's hurt.

Jimmy looks at Hayley. They shrug at each other.

ED: Aren't you going to do something? 30

JIMMY: I'm not a doctor. Angels don't do first aid. You need to report it to the office.

ED: But … but … you need to do something. You need to—

HAYLEY: Are you telling us what we should do? Do 35 you know something we don't? Do you know anything about anything? Or are you just some smelly little kid who's crawled out of the Bin?

JIMMY: *We* decide when – and how – we do what 40 we do. Clear?

ED: *(Quietly)* Clear.

JIMMY: And what do you do?

ED: *(Quietly)* I do what I'm told.

JIMMY: So go to the office and tell them. OK? 45

Exit Ed and Shane.

Enter Anika and Ollie, closely followed by Sean and Aidan.

Sean and Aidan are wearing orange armbands.

One by one, Jimmy, Hayley and Harry notice and stare as they approach.

Anika and Ollie think they are staring at them – then realise and stare at Sean and Aidan.

As everyone stares, Aidan seems to be enjoying the attention while Sean's embarrassment grows.

SEAN: Alright?

HAYLEY: *(Pointing to Sean's armband)* Funny. Ha. Ha.

JIMMY: What are you doing? You're really pushing it now, boys. D'you know what the penalty is for impersonating an Angel?   50

AIDAN: No. What is it?

Pause.

JIMMY: I dunno. But it's not good. About a year in the Bin?

HARRY: *(Indicating Sean's and Aidan's armbands)* Where did you get those from?

AIDAN: We've just seen Mr Stone. He gave them us.   55

HAYLEY: Are you joking? They've actually made you an Angel?

AIDAN: Go and ask him if you like. Mr Stone said we'd make really good Angels. Didn't he, Sean?

SEAN: Yeah.   60

AIDAN: Good, innit?

JIMMY: Unbelievable …

SEAN: *(Grinning)* We're just like you now, Jimmy.

JIMMY: I am *nothing* like you two.

SEAN: But we're all on the same side now. We're 65
one big, happy family.

AIDAN: *(Aggressively)* Gotta problem?

SEAN: Leave it, Aid.

AIDAN: *(Spinning round to all)* Anyone got a problem?
(To Amy) You! What you staring at? Never 70
seen an Angel before?

Aidan marches aggressively towards Amy.

Exit Amy, running.

AIDAN: Come back here!

*Exit Aidan, running after Amy. There is the sound
of Amy being hurt.*

SEAN: He's keen, isn't he? Straight to work, no
messing. Gotta admire him for it.

JIMMY: I think it's wrong. 75

SEAN: What?

JIMMY: No, I think it's *disgusting*.

SEAN: What?

JIMMY: Well … nothing personal, Sean, but I don't
think someone who's been in the Bin 80
should get to be an Angel. It doesn't make
sense.

SEAN: Why?

HAYLEY: If you don't get it, then you shouldn't be an
          Angel.   85

SEAN: Oh, I get it. I get what you're saying. You
          think I can't do it. You think I'm too bad. You
          think I can't change. Well, we'll see, won't
          we. We'll see.

          Exit Sean.

JESS: This is mad.   90

JIMMY: It just ruins it for the rest of us. If they let
          people like that get the armband, then it
          makes us all look like Binners. What's the
          difference between me and Sean now?

JESS: No, not that. The whole thing. It's just mad.   95

JIMMY: What do you mean?

JESS: It's out of control. Can't you see that?

JIMMY: Sean and Aidan won't last. They're not
          Angels. They're Binners. They'll slip up, you
          watch. They'll—   100

JESS: No, not that. It's not just that. It's *everything*.
          Angels were supposed to be extra eyes and
          ears for teachers. But now they're running
          the school. No one does anything without an
          Angel's say so. Kids don't get sent to the   105
          Bin, they get to do little jobs for Angels,
          running round after them like servants, like
          slaves. And then they give Aidan an armband
          so now he can go round hitting kids and it
          doesn't matter, cos no one'll say anything.   110
          They're scared they'll get binned. And who
          knows what happens in there? The only

people who do know are too scared to say.
It's got to stop. It's got to stop.

HAYLEY: Finished? 115

JESS: For now.

ANIKA: She's right.

JIMMY: So what are you saying?

JESS: I'm saying we need to stop doing it. Give up.
Give the armband back. Resign. All of us. 120

HAYLEY: *(In disbelief)* What?

JIMMY: You think you're going to get every Angel to
give it up?

JESS: It's the only way to stop it. They can't do it if
they haven't got any Angels, can they? 125

HAYLEY: You think people are gonna give it up just
cos you don't like it? A lot of people happen
to think it's really good.

JESS: Yeah, a lot of people like *you* who get off on
bossing people around and having a bit of 130
power over kids who are scared of getting
binned. You think they're scared of you and
it makes you feel big. But it's not you they're
scared of. It's the system. And the system
stinks. 135

HAYLEY: Oh, shut up, Jess. You don't know what
you're talking about.

HARRY: I'm not giving it up. I like it.

HAYLEY: You wanna watch what you say, Jess. If you
talk like that and word gets round, you'll 140
end up in a big pile of trouble.

JIMMY: And it won't work. People won't give it up.
          They think it works. They think it's good. A
          lot of people out there are much happier cos
          of what we do.   145

          Harry, Hayley and Jimmy start to leave.

JIMMY: It's good for everyone.

          Exit Harry, Hayley and Jimmy.

          Blackout.

Scene 3

*Enter Ed and Shane in their orange Binner t-shirts.
They sit and look fed up.*

Pause.

SHANE: Wanna go up the canteen?

ED: No.

SHANE: Game of footie?

ED: No.

SHANE: I know! What about—   5

ED: I don't want to do anything and I don't want
          to go anywhere, OK?

SHANE: That's what I love about you, mate. You're
          such fun to be with.

ED: I'm just … sick of this.   10

SHANE: Sick of what?

ED: *(Grabbing his t-shirt)* This.

SHANE: It's not that bad.

ED: Isn't it? You like running around after Harry, do you? You like doing whatever he says, 15 whatever he wants, whenever he wants it?

SHANE: It's better than going back in the Bin. Anything's better than that.

Enter Kyle and Bradley.

KYLE: Look, Brad. There are some bad children! Some naughty children! 20

ED: *(Sarcastically)* Ha ha.

BRADLEY: Don't be scared, Kyle. The Angels will protect us from the bad children.

KYLE: But these two look so dangerous!

BRADLEY: Are you *very* dangerous? 25

ED: Yeah. Deadly.

Enter Jimmy and Harry. They stand and stare at Shane and Ed.

JIMMY: What are you doing?

Shane jumps up; Ed stays sitting.

ED: Sitting down. You?

JIMMY: I'll tell you what I'm doing. I'll tell you, shall I? I'm looking for you. I've been looking for 30 you for ten minutes. I've got a job for you.

BRADLEY: A job?

JIMMY: Shut up, Bradley.

HARRY: Come on, Shane.

Shane stands and goes to Harry.

JIMMY:	*(To Ed)* I thought we'd got this clear, Ed. I thought we understood each other. I tell you what to do – and what do you do?	35
ED:	*(Quietly)* I do what I'm told.	
BRADLEY:	Hang on, hang on. Explain that to me again, Jimmy. Bit slower this time. I'm not sure I believe what I'm hearing.	40
JIMMY:	Shut up, Bradley. Are you doing what you're told, Ed? *(He gets out his phone)* Or do you need some encouragement?	
KYLE:	What does a bully look like, Jimmy?	45
JIMMY:	Eh?	
KYLE:	What does a bully look like?	
JIMMY:	I don't know, Kyle. What does a bully look like?	
KYLE:	About your height. Same colour hair. Same—	
JIMMY:	That's very funny, Kyle. Ed, come here.	50
BRADLEY:	Don't do it, Ed. You're not his servant. You're not his slave. You don't have to do jobs for him.	
JIMMY:	*(Texting)* Last warning, Ed.	
ED:	*(Quietly)* I'm not doing it.	
JIMMY:	You're going back to the Bin. You know that, don't you?	55
ED:	No, I'm not.	
KYLE:	Oh, come on, Jimmy, you don't have to do that. OK, so you're a great big important Angel. Doesn't mean you have to push him around, does it?	60
HARRY:	Come on, Ed. Be sensible.	

JIMMY: I'm sending it …

KYLE: Come on, Jimmy, he's just …

JIMMY: *(With a final look at Ed)* Now. *(To Kyle and* 65
Bradley) You still here?

The loudspeakers crackle.

VOICE 1: Attention. This is a disciplinary
announcement. Attention. This is a
disciplinary announcement. Would …

VOICE 2: … Edward Mills … 70

VOICE 1: … please make your way to the
Rehabilitation Unit.

ED: *(Quietly)* I'm not going.

JIMMY: What?

ED: I'm not going. I'm not going back there. To 75
the Bin. I'm not going.

VOICE 2: Edward Mills.

VOICE 1: You have two minutes to make your way to
the Rehabilitation Unit.

JIMMY: Can you hear that, Ed? Can you hear what 80
they're saying? You've gotta go.

ED: Can you hear me, Jimmy? I'm not going.

BRADLEY: *(Triumphantly)* Yeah, what are you gonna do
now, Angels?

VOICE 2: Edward Mills. 85

VOICE 1: You have been placed in the Rehabilitation
Unit for one day. Failure to attend promptly
will result in your placement being extended.
You have less than two minutes to report to
the Rehabilitation Unit. 90

Ed folds his arms defiantly and remains sitting.

Jimmy and Harry look at each other, at Ed and back to each other again.

HARRY: *(To Jimmy)* What do we do?

JIMMY: I … we …

HARRY: Should I tell someone? Shall I go and find Mr Stone?

JIMMY: And make me look a right idiot? No, he's 95 going to the Bin. He's going. Get up, Ed! Get up!

Ed stares defiantly back at Jimmy.

JIMMY: Get up, Ed! Get up!

Ed continues to stare. Jimmy loses patience and grabs Ed. Ed screams and struggles as Jimmy starts half-dragging, half-carrying him away.

BRADLEY: Hang on, hang on.

Bradley goes to intervene. Harry places himself between Bradley and Jimmy, brandishing his phone.

HARRY: Don't touch him! 100

Bradley backs away, hands held up defensively.

VOICE 2: Edward Mills.

VOICE 1: You have one minute to report to the Rehabilitation Unit.

Exit Jimmy carrying/dragging Ed, who still struggles.

Harry avoids Bradley's and Kyle's stares.

HARRY: Come on, Shane.

Exit Harry and Shane in the other direction, with just one glance back at Kyle and Bradley.

Blackout.

Scene 4

Breaktime a couple of days later.

*A bell rings. Enter Jimmy, Hayley, Harry, Sean and Aidan. They stand centre stage, **imposingly**.*

Nothing happens.

AIDAN: So this is what it's like, is it? This is being an Angel?

JIMMY: What's going on? Where is everyone?

A group of students wander in, whispering feverishly. Something has happened. They skirt round the Angels, clearly avoiding them.

Enter Amy, running, obviously in a hurry to be somewhere.

HAYLEY: Oi! Amy! Come here.

Amy pauses for a moment, looks at Hayley and exits, running.

HAYLEY: What the ...? What's going on?   5

Enter Shane and Nav, running.

HAYLEY: Shane? *(He pauses. Nav slows reluctantly)* What's going on?

SHANE:	*(Panting; anxiously)* Haven't you heard? He's dead.
JIMMY:	What? 10
HARRY:	Who's dead?
SHANE:	Ed.
JIMMY:	What?
SHANE:	He got binned yesterday – and he never came out at the end of school. So I waited 15 and waited and waited and I gave up and went home. I came in this morning and he's not here.
JIMMY:	He's probably ill. Or says he is.
SHANE:	No, he's dead. They said he dropped down 20 dead in the Bin.
HARRY:	Who said?
SHANE:	Everyone.

Exit Shane and Nav, running.

HAYLEY:	That's rubbish. It's a story. The kid's sitting at home watching TV telling his mum his 25 tummy hurts.
JIMMY:	And what if he isn't? What if he is … dead?
HAYLEY:	'Course he isn't.

Enter Jess, Anika and Ollie.

ANIKA:	Is it true?
HAYLEY:	Is what true? 30
ANIKA:	They're saying some kid died in the Bin.
HAYLEY:	'Course it isn't true. Believe everything you hear in this place, do you?

JIMMY: *(Distantly, to Anika)* I put him in there. I binned him. *(Pause)* He's dead and it's my fault. 35

HAYLEY: Shut up, Jimmy. No one died.

JESS: Hayley, you're all heart.

Enter Beth and Jade. They peer closely at Hayley's, Harry's and Jimmy's faces.

JADE: *(Triumphantly)* Look at them! Look at their faces! I told you it was true! I told you I saw an ambulance! 40

BETH: I knew it was true anyway. Cos my cousin lives over the road from him and she said he had a fit or something. Fell over. Died.

JADE: Who binned him? 45

Hayley, Harry and Jimmy exchange glances.

BETH: They've gone all quiet. Who was it?

JIMMY: *(Quietly)* Me.

JADE: Well, it's your fault then, isn't it?

HAYLEY: Shut up, Jade, just shut up!

JADE: I'm just saying … 50

JIMMY: She's right. If I hadn't binned him, he wouldn't have died. It is my fault. I might as well have killed him. What am I gonna do? What'll happen to me?

JADE: I expect the police'll want a word. They usually do. 55

HAYLEY: Look. Even if he is dead – which he probably isn't – but even if he is, it's not our problem.

People die all the time. It doesn't mean it's
anyone's fault.   60

*Jade notices Sean and Aidan are wearing
armbands.*

JADE: Oh my God, Sean, what have you got on
your arm? They haven't!

SEAN: *(Grinning)* They have. I'm an Angel.

AIDAN: *(Grinning)* And me.

JADE: Not for long, mate. I heard this is the end of 65
it. I heard they're getting rid of the Bin now
this kid's died.

HAYLEY: What?

JADE: That's what I heard.

Enter Bradley and Kyle.

BRADLEY: You heard? About the dead kid?   70

KYLE: It's all coming down. Falling down around us.

BRADLEY: They're shutting the Bin.

KYLE: Getting rid of the Angels. You heard that?

BRADLEY: You're out of a job.

KYLE: On the scrap heap.   75

BRADLEY: Gotta give your little wings and halo back.

Enter Amy and a crowd of five or six students.

KYLE: *(To the students)* Oi, come here. *(He points at
the Angels)* See them?

The students eye the Angels warily.

KYLE: You can do what you like to them.

He pokes Jimmy with a finger. Jimmy looks to the other Angels for support, they look away anxiously.

HAYLEY: Watch it, Kyle.   80

KYLE: *(Imitating her)* Watch it, Kyle. *(He starts circling the Angels)* I told you. It's gone midnight. The magic's over.

The students join in with the circling and jeering. More students arrive and join in.

BRADLEY: *(Poking each Angel in turn)* You … you … you … you … and you … are *(he goes round again)* … out … out … out … out … out.   85

The students take up the chant.

STUDENTS: Out, out, out …

*Bradley, Kyle and the other students start to close in. The Angels look nervously at each other, except Aidan who glares angrily and steadily at his **taunters**.*

STUDENTS: Out, out, out …

All the Angels except Aidan are pushed back by the approaching mob. Aidan stands his ground and ends up face to face with Bradley – and headbutts him. Bradley falls to the ground.

There is sudden silence and everyone stops moving.

OLLIE: Two dead, nine hundred and ninety-eight to go.   90

AIDAN: *(Pulling out his phone)* I'm going to start counting. Any of you lot still standing here by the time I get to ten are binned.

The mob look at each other.

AIDAN: One … two …

Some students start to drift away.

AMY: *(To Kyle)* You said it was over! You said the   95
Angels were finished.

AIDAN: He lied. 'Course, anyone who wants to take a gamble can stay. But you need to ask yourselves: have they really shut the Bin down? Or is it just a story? Think about it.   100
And while you're doing that, I'm still counting. Three … four …

The students quickly disperse but Kyle stands firm.

AIDAN: *(Beginning to text on his phone)* Five … six … seven … eight … nine … ten … 'Send'. *(He pushes the button on the phone with a flourish)*

Pause. Kyle and Aidan stand face to face. Kyle starts to smile.

The loudspeakers crackle.

VOICE 1: Attention. This is a disciplinary   105
announcement. Attention. This is a disciplinary announcement. Would …

VOICE 2: … Kyle Bennett and Bradley Harper …

VOICE 1: … please make your way to the Rehabilitation Unit.   110

As the voices drone on, Aidan smiles, starts to laugh, then laughs more and more until he is laughing uncontrollably. Kyle helps Bradley up and they exit.

VOICE 2: Kyle Bennett and Bradley Harper.

VOICE 1: You have two minutes to make your way to the Rehabilitation Unit.

VOICE 2: Kyle Bennett and Bradley Harper.

VOICE 1: You have been placed in the Rehabilitation 115 Unit for one day. Failure to attend promptly will result in your placement being extended. You have less than two minutes to report to the Rehabilitation Unit.

VOICE 2: Kyle Bennett and Bradley Harper. 120

VOICE 1: You have one minute to report to the Rehabilitation Unit.

Blackout.

Scene 5

Breaktime the following day.

A bell rings. Enter Jimmy, Sean, Aidan, Hayley and Harry, walking and talking, followed by Ed, Shane and Nav at a respectful distance.

JIMMY: One stupid story and it all falls apart.

HARRY: He's not dead then, that kid?

HAYLEY: 'Course he's not dead. *(She turns to Ed)* Are you?

Ed shakes his head.

HAYLEY: Weren't even ill, were you?

ED:	*(Showing his teeth)* **Orthodontist**.	5
HAYLEY:	Beautiful. *(To Jimmy)* See? Everything's fine.	
JIMMY:	But it was like … one minute you think you've got everything under control and the next … the next minute they turn on you.	
SEAN:	*(Snapping his fingers)* Like that.	10
JIMMY:	Makes you think, doesn't it?	
HAYLEY:	Gotta keep the faith, Jimmy. Gotta believe.	
AIDAN:	Gotta take control. Gotta keep strong. Let them see you're strong. Let them know they're weak.	15

Aidan cuffs Ed round the back of the head. Ed follows him, regardless.

HAYLEY:	You losing the faith, Jimmy?	
JIMMY:	*(Uncertainly)* No, 'course not.	

Enter Anika, Jess and Ollie, walking towards the Angels. Jess is no longer wearing her armband.

As they meet, Jimmy looks pleased to see them. Hayley, Harry, Aidan and the others walk on and exit. Sean hangs back with Jimmy.

ANIKA:	You alright, Jimmy?	
JIMMY:	Yeah, couldn't be better.	
JESS:	Loving the life of an Angel?	20
JIMMY:	'Course. Nothing better. Best ever. Can't beat it!	
JESS:	Really?	

Pause.

JIMMY:	No … *(To Jess)* Where's your armband?

JESS: Gave it back.

JIMMY: You what?   25

JESS: Gave it back.

JIMMY: You mean …?

JESS: Yup. Not an Angel any more.

JIMMY: What did he say?

JESS: Mr Stone? He just said it was a shame and it   30
doesn't suit everyone and blah, blah, blah. I
told him I thought the whole system stinks.

SEAN: What did he say?

JESS: Pretended to care. Asked me why. Said he'd
take my comments on board.   35

SEAN: What does that mean?

JESS: Means he's forgotten them already.

Pause.

JESS: You don't have to do it, Jimmy. You can get
out now. I saw what happened yesterday.
How long will it be before Aidan kills   40
someone?

SEAN: I thought he *had* killed Bradley.

JESS: How long before you end up doing
something you regret?

Pause.

JIMMY: I thought I'd killed that kid yesterday.   45

SEAN: It's wrong. All of it. It's all wrong.

JESS: You going to give the armband back then,
Jimmy?

JIMMY: What difference would it make? If it's not me, it'll be someone else. 50

JESS: And what if everyone gave it up?

SEAN: It won't happen. They all love it, don't they, Hayley and that lot?

JESS: But if we can persuade enough people to give it up … if we can persuade half the 55 Angels to give it up, it'll fall apart. They can't run it if there aren't enough of them.

JIMMY: If I did give it up … if we could stop it … what would happen? What would it be like?

JESS: I don't know but it's gotta be better than this, 60 hasn't it? And this is getting worse. Look at it now. What's it going to be like in a week, a month? What's it going to be like next year?

Pause.

JIMMY: OK. How are we gonna do it?

Pause.

ANIKA: *(Checking her phone)* The bell's going to go 65 any minute. We'll meet back here at lunch-time and talk about it. OK?

OLLIE: A plan! How exciting. It's like being in the Famous Five.

ANIKA: Keep it quiet. Not a word to anyone. OK? 70

They nod. The bell rings and they exit.

Blackout.

Scene 6

Later at lunch-time.

Enter Jimmy. He stands nervously, looking out for the others.

Enter Sean. After a brief nod, they stand uncomfortably for a few seconds, avoiding eye contact.

Enter Jess, Anika and Ollie.

JESS: Alright?

Pause.

OLLIE: So. What are we gonna do?

JIMMY: I've been thinking. Mass protest. Get everyone – all the Angels, the Binners, everyone – refusing to go to lessons. Get 5 the word round. Everyone meets up outside school tomorrow morning. If enough people turn up, they won't be able to control it.

JESS: And what if we're the only ones who do it? We end up in the Bin for the rest of our lives 10 and nothing changes.

SEAN: We need to be a bit sly. A bit careful.

ANIKA: Wait, wait, wait. You saw what Aidan was like with Bradley yesterday. If all the Angels were like that, they'd have to stop it. Wouldn't 15 they? They couldn't let that happen, could they?

JIMMY: So we persuade all the Angels to go round acting like psychopaths?

ANIKA:	Yeah, they'd have to shut it down.	20
JIMMY:	So we all start hurting people and then … wait for something to happen?	
JESS:	And how long would that take? How many people do we have to damage before they shut it down?	25
JIMMY:	And maybe that's what they want. Maybe that's what they think will make us all be good and quiet and nice.	
ANIKA:	So that wasn't my best ever idea – but it was my *only* idea.	30

Pause.

OLLIE:	What about if loads of Angels start being bad – on purpose I mean – and get binned. That'd be amazing! Half the Angels binning the other half! There'd be hardly any Angels left and they'd look really bad cos—	35
SEAN:	Who's gonna do that? I'm not going back in there. You haven't been binned. You don't know what it's like.	
JESS:	What happens if an Angel reports another Angel?	40
SEAN:	Dunno, it's never been done. Not yet, anyway.	
OLLIE:	Exciting! What d'you reckon?	
JIMMY:	There must be something we can do.	
OLLIE:	Oh, thanks for giving my idea your full attention, everyone.	45
JIMMY:	No one's going to get themselves binned on purpose, Ollie.	

ANIKA:	What happened yesterday? A story goes round that someone has died and everyone goes mad. I mean, they weren't frightened any more. They were treating Angels like they were nothing.
JESS:	That's cos they thought it was over. They thought they weren't going to get binned cos there was no Bin any more. So they didn't care.
JIMMY:	But if everyone in the school did that – if no one took any notice of the Angels – they couldn't bin everyone, could they? It'd fall apart. It'd be the end of it.
JESS:	So what do we do? Kill someone?
ANIKA:	Or fake it?
SEAN:	No, it just needs one person. One person to stand up and say what everyone's thinking.
JIMMY:	Yeah, we just need to stir it up. Say what everyone's thinking. They're too scared to say it – so we need to say it for them. And if we start saying it, they might start saying it too. If we get enough people saying it, the Angels won't be able to do anything.
ANIKA:	What if Aidan starts nutting people again?
JIMMY:	It won't matter. There'll be too many of us. He can't nut all of us.
SEAN:	*(Smiling)* You sure about that?
OLLIE:	So what do we do exactly?
JIMMY:	Talk to people.
OLLIE:	And what do we say? We hate the Angels so let's have a riot?

JIMMY: No, we just ask them if they're happy with
the Angels thing. 80

OLLIE: And if they say 'Yeah'?

JIMMY: Then you say 'Me too, I love 'em'.

OLLIE: And if they say 'No'?

JIMMY: Then tell them to come and talk to us and …
well, I dunno. Let's see how many people 85
turn up and see what happens. OK?

There is general agreement.

JIMMY: So that's it. Talk to as many people as you
can and get them to meet here at lunch-time
tomorrow. Say, half one? That way we've got
a bit of time to get a few more people. 90

They nod and get ready to move.

ANIKA: Be careful who you talk to. And talk quietly.

All exit in different directions.

Blackout.

Scene 7

Lunch-time the following day.

*As the lights come up, a large group of people are
already on stage: Sean, Hayley, Harry, Aidan, Nav,
Ed, Shane, Amy, Beth, Jade, Kyle, Bradley. They
look on silently and expectantly as events unfold.*

*Enter Jimmy. He looks pleased at the size of the
crowd.*

JIMMY: You've done well, Sean.

SEAN: *(Smiling)* Thanks, Jimmy.

As Jimmy looks at the individual members of the crowd, a tone of nervousness creeps into his voice.

JIMMY: And they're all … I mean they think the same as we do?

SEAN: Oh, yeah. I think we all agree what needs to   5
be done.

Enter Jess, Ollie and Anika from different directions.

OLLIE: Well, it's not exactly a riot but it's a start, I s'pose.

JIMMY: *(To Jess, Anika and Ollie)* How did you get on?

JESS: Not great. A lot of people are too scared to   10
say anything – let alone do something. A
couple of people said they might come but I
dunno.

ANIKA: *(Looking at the crowd; to Jimmy)* Did you get all
of this lot?   15

JIMMY: No, Sean did. I got a couple of 'maybes' and—

ANIKA: I can't believe some of the Angels are here. I
mean … Aidan? Hayley? Something's not
right. Something's—

SEAN: So, Jimmy. D'you wanna tell everyone why   20
we're here?

ANIKA: *(Whispering urgently)* Jimmy!

JIMMY: *(To Sean)* Er … yeah. OK. *(To all)* The thing
is … we think … that is, some of us have a
problem with the whole Angels thing.   25

SEAN: And what is that problem, Jimmy?

| JIMMY: | We think that … er … the Angels have got too much power … and that it's not being used how it should be. And the Bin. That's another thing. The Bin's just … wrong. | 30 |

| SEAN: | So what do you think we should do about it, Jimmy? | |

| JIMMY: | Well … we think that all the Angels should say they don't want to do it any more … *if* they don't want to do it any more … you know, we're not forcing anyone to do anything they don't want to do, cos then we'd be like the Angels are, forcing people to do stuff they don't want to do – I mean, not all of them … just some of them. But if you think, er … if you agree with us, then we think we should get together and fight. | 35

40 |

| SEAN: | Fight what, Jimmy? | |

| JIMMY: | Well, the system, I s'pose. The whole … Angels system. | 45 |

There is an embarrassingly long silence.

| SEAN: | But that's wrong, isn't it, Jimmy? | |

| JIMMY: | What? | |

| SEAN: | What you're saying. It's wrong. You're putting the success of this school in danger. You're undermining school discipline. Well, that can't be allowed to happen, can it? This school needs Angels. *(Pause)* Bin him, Hayley. | 50 |

| HAYLEY: | Seems like we've got no choice. | |

Hayley gets out her phone and sends a text.

JIMMY: What … what are you doing?

SEAN: I'm doing what Angels do, Jimmy. I'm 55
keeping things how they should be. I'm
keeping people like you out of trouble. Now
where have I heard that before?

*As before, the prerecorded voices come over the
loudspeakers.*

VOICE 1: Attention. This is a disciplinary
announcement. Attention. This is a 60
disciplinary announcement. Would …

VOICE 2: … Jimmy Hope …

VOICE 1: … please make your way to the
Rehabilitation Unit.

SEAN: And these three. *(He indicates Jess, Anika* 65
and Ollie) They were all in it with him.

*Hayley sends more texts. Slowly the crowd gathers
around Jimmy, Anika, Jess and Ollie.*

SEAN: Time's running out, Jimmy. So here's a little
tip for you. The quicker you get yourself to
the Bin, the better. The slower you get there,
the more it hurts, Jimmy. It really hurts. 70
You see, I know, Jimmy. Cos I've been
binned. D'you remember?

JIMMY: But you said it was wrong. You said Angels
were wrong. You lied to me, Sean, you lied.

SEAN: Oh, I don't think so. I never lie. For 75
example, remember what I said to you when
you binned me, Jimmy?

JIMMY: No.

SEAN: You should have listened more carefully. You should have taken notice. You should have 80 paid attention.

JIMMY: *(Reluctantly)* You said I'd be sorry. You said I'd wish I'd never been born.

SEAN: Was I lying? No. I never lie. If I say you'll be sorry, you *will* be sorry. 85

VOICE 2: Jimmy Hope, Jessica Wright, Anika Howarth and Oliver Burton.

VOICE 1: You have two minutes to make your way to the Rehabilitation Unit.

SEAN: Funny thing is, Jimmy, you thought this was 90 the end of it, didn't you? But this is just the beginning.

JESS: Beginning?

SEAN: Yeah, the beginning. Well, we couldn't carry on like we were, could we? Something had 95 to happen. Look at me and Aidan here. We were running wild, doing whatever we wanted, didn't care. Well, that had to stop. People need discipline. People need rules. People *like* rules. And if someone breaks 100 the rules, people like to see them punished. They like to see them get what they deserve.

VOICE 2: Jimmy Hope, Jessica Wright, Anika Howarth and Oliver Burton.

VOICE 1: You have one minute to report to the 105 Rehabilitation Unit.

SEAN: And it works. Just one visit to the Bin and I'm reformed. I'm one of the good guys. You

should thank me, Jimmy. You should thank
me for saving you. *(To Jess, Anika and Ollie)*   110
All of you should.

VOICE 2:   Jimmy Hope, Jessica Wright, Anika Howarth
and Oliver Burton.

VOICE 1:   You have thirty seconds to report to the
Rehabilitation Unit.   115

OLLIE: We'd better go.

JIMMY: I'm not going.

JESS: You've got no choice, Jimmy. None of us have.

JIMMY: I tell you, I'm not going. I'm not going just
cos this Binner wants to get his own back.   120
It's not right. This isn't what I deserve. I just
wanted to make things better. I just wanted
to make things how they should be.

SEAN: Let me help you, Jimmy. Just to make sure
you get there safely. Aid?   125

*Aidan and Sean place themselves either side of
Jimmy.*

JIMMY: *(To Sean)* Alright, alright. I'm going. I'm going
to the Bin. But you need to know. It should
be you in there. Not me. Not me.

Jimmy walks away, then turns on Sean.

JIMMY: This isn't the beginning. This is the end.
Understand? This is the end.   130

Blackout.

Scene 8

Continued from the opening scene: a single
spotlight is on Jimmy. He is talking to the dark,
disturbing, adult voice again.

VOICE: This is just the beginning, Jimmy. Do you see?

Silence.

VOICE: Do … you … see?

JIMMY: Yes.

VOICE: Good. The system works, Jimmy. The system
must work. And I am responsible for its   5
success.

Silence.

VOICE: And that's why I must insist on absolute
dedication. No second thoughts. No doubts.
No questions. An Angel who does not believe
in what they are doing is no use to me. Do   10
you see?

Silence.

VOICE: Do … you … see?

JIMMY: Yes.

VOICE: Recently some students were led to believe
that a boy had died during rehabilitation.   15
These students believed the system had
failed and was being shut down. As a result
their behaviour and attitude to Angels
became entirely unacceptable. Fortunately,
due to the foresight of one Angel, the   20
situation was brought under control. But you

81

see even the smallest weakness, the smallest failing cannot be permitted. We must all have faith in the system or the system fails.

Pause.

VOICE: I have received several reports of your recent activities, Jimmy. 25

JIMMY: Yes, all of them from Sean Sutton. He's just trying to—

VOICE: From *several* sources, Jimmy. You are a person with influence in this school. A 30 dangerous influence. Already you have persuaded your friends of your views.

JIMMY: Where are my friends? Where are Jess and Ollie and Anika?

VOICE: They're currently in the Rehabilitation Unit. 35

JIMMY: Is that where I'm going?

VOICE: Unfortunately no, Jimmy. I'm afraid that's not possible. As you know, someone who has been in the Rehabilitation Unit – or the Bin as I believe some people call it – someone 40 who has been in the Bin can prove themselves reformed and become an Angel. Like Sean Sutton, for example.

JIMMY: Ha!

VOICE: However, it doesn't work the other way 45 round. An Angel cannot be sent for rehabilitation. It would … lower their status. The respect other students have for them would be destroyed.

| JIMMY: | What's going to happen then? What are you going to do to me? | 50 |

| VOICE: | I'm afraid, Jimmy, that you cannot be allowed to spread your views any further. Your influence cannot be allowed to undermine and destroy all that we have achieved. | 55 |

Pause.

| VOICE: | Important people are watching us, Jimmy. Important people are waiting for the Angels programme to succeed. And it will succeed. Because when – and I mean *when* – it has run successfully for a year, it will be introduced in every school in the country. Do you know who has been asked to organise this, Jimmy? Do you know who has been entrusted with this enormous responsibility? | 60 ... 65 |

Pause.

| VOICE: | Me. Therefore, an attack on the Angels programme is an attack on me, Jimmy. When you and your views endanger the success of the Angels programme, you are endangering my future, the school's future, the future of every young person in this country. I'm afraid, Jimmy, that you cannot be allowed to continue. I'm afraid, Jimmy, that you will have to be removed from the school. | 70 |

| JIMMY: | You mean expelled? | 75 |

| VOICE: | In a way, Jimmy. In a way. You will leave the school now. You will walk home. You will do |

this without the school's permission. You will simply walk out. Perhaps you felt you had to get out because you failed to persuade others to join your little campaign.

80

JIMMY: *(Panicking slightly)* And then what?

Silence.

JIMMY: What do you mean?

Silence.

JIMMY: And what if I won't go? What if I say no?

VOICE: Then we will have to encourage you to go.

85

Pause.

VOICE: You have two minutes, Jimmy, in which to do as you have been asked. You have two minutes to leave the school grounds. Start walking, Jimmy. It's time to go.

Blackout.

The End

Glossary

amputation cutting off, as in an operation to remove a limb
anticipation looking forward to something happening
audible can be heard
bickering squabbling
deft quick and skilful
flinching shrinking back from something in pain or fear
fluorescent shiny and luminous in the dark
imposingly commandingly
inaudible cannot be heard
indignant angry at the actions or words of another
King Kong a gorilla-like monster who first appeared in the 1933 film of this name
mocking mimicking or teasing in an unkind way
orthodontist specialist dentist
relentlessly without stopping
reluctantly unwillingly
sarcastically sneeringly or scornfully
taunter someone who makes repeated unpleasant remarks or jokes about someone to their face to annoy them
taunting making repeated unpleasant remarks or jokes about someone to their face to annoy them
vulnerable capable of being hurt

Activities

Activity 1: Predictions

Before you read the play

> You will:
>
> - explore different meanings and interpretations of the word 'angel'
> - predict what *Angels* might be about
>
> You will do this by considering the different characteristics of angels and how these characteristics have often been portrayed.

1 **Work with a partner.** The title of the play is *Angels*. Can you think of any other examples of angels in religion, cinema or art? Put them in a table like the one below.

Angels in religion	Angels in cinema	Angels in art
• In Islam, believing in angels is one of the Six Articles of Faith	• In *Constantine* (2005), the character Constantine can communicate with angels	• Michelangelo painted many angels in the Sistine Chapel

2 **Work on your own.** Draw an outline of an angel. Fill the wings with a list of all the characteristics you understand angels to have.

3 Consider the information you wrote down for tasks 1 and 2. Bearing this information in mind, write down answers to the following questions:

   - What do you think the play *Angels* will be about?
   - What kind of angels do you think the play will contain?

4 Keep the angel you drew for task 2 until you finish reading the play. You can then return to the angel and tick off all the characteristics that were demonstrated by angels in the play and add any further characteristics you've found the angels in the play to have around the outside of the drawing.

Activity 2: Silent argument

After reading Act One, Scene 1

You will:

- compare your ideas about discipline in school

You will do this by having a silent argument about discipline in schools.

1   On a large piece of paper, have one student write the statement 'Discipline in schools is not very good these days'. Then put this piece of paper on a table at the front of the class.

2   **Work in groups.** Try to come up with as many responses to the original statement as possible. Each group will then have 30 seconds to write their comments on the piece of paper at the front of the class. This must be done in *absolute silence*.

3   **Work as a class.** After each group has written their comments onto the silent argument sheet, review the comments together. What was the general response to the statement? You can display this in your classroom to fuel discussions as you continue to read the play.

Activity 3: School report

After reading Act One, Scenes 2–4

You will:

• explore the character of Sean Sutton

You will do this by reading Act One, Scenes 2–4 and writing a school report.

1 **Work on your own.** Carefully read Act One, Scenes 2–4. Fill in a table like the one below. Write down any quotes in which the character Sean is making fun of others.

Line references	Insults from Sean

2 **Work with a partner.** Discuss what sort of student Sean is. What reasons can you think of for him acting the way he does?

3 **Work on your own.** Imagine you are Sean's teacher. Write a school report for him. Include the following:

• a written paragraph and scores out of 10 for each of the following: effort, behaviour and motivation;

• a paragraph about Sean's social life at school, including who his friends are and how he interacts with them;

• suggestions for any improvements Sean could make in class.

Activity 4: Role play

After reading Act Two, Scene 1

You will:

- explore the character of Jimmy Hope

You will do this by preparing a role play between the Angels and the other students.

1 **Work with a partner.** Read Act Two, Scene 1 very carefully. Discuss the following:

- How has Jimmy changed?
- How might this affect the friendships he currently has?

2 Join another pair to **work as a group.** Create a short role play to show an incident where some of Jimmy's friends have misbehaved. Think carefully about how to show the following:

- Jimmy's reaction to the incident and his course of action;
- how Jimmy's relationship with his friends has changed.

3 **Work on your own.** Imagine that Anika and Ollie write notes to one another during class, and today they are writing about the change in Jimmy's behaviour. Write down three notes that Anika and Ollie might send to each other. Try to show their opinions on the change in Jimmy and their opinions on the Angels and what they are doing.

Activity 5: Extra scene

After reading Act Two, Scenes 1–2

> You will:
>
> • explore the idea of student punishment
>
> You will do this by writing an additional scene that takes place in the Bin.

1 **Work as a class**. Read Act Two, Scenes 1–2. Make a list of all the things you believe happen in the 'Sin Bin'.

2 **Work with a partner.** Make a list of ideas for school punishments. Create a table like the one below to record your ideas. Be prepared to share your best ideas with the class.

Misbehaviour	Punishment

3 **Work on your own.** Write a new scene about a student's trip to the Bin. Your scene should give an idea of what happens in the Bin, taking into consideration all of the reactions that you've read about the Bin so far in the play.

Activity 6: A new voice

After reading Act Two, Scene 3

You will:

- think about the Angels from the point of view of the younger students

You will do this by writing a new scene for the play.

1 **Work on your own.** Read through Act Two, Scene 3.

2 **Work with a partner.** Discuss what the younger students in the play might say about the Angels when they are not around.

3 Come up with an idea for a new scene for the play. Your new scene should involve at least two of the younger students discussing how they feel about the Angels.

4 Write a script for your scene, being sure to make us aware of the younger students' perspectives in the play. Think carefully about how they might respond to what has happened so far, their feelings towards the Angels and those who have been 'Binned', their attitudes towards the 'powers that be' within the school, etc.

5 Perform your scene to the class. Allow others to assess your performance and give feedback about its effectiveness. Remember to be positive when assessing others' performances.

Activity 7: Being Jimmy

After reading Act Two, Scene 4 to Act Three, Scene 2

> You will:
> - explore how Jimmy has changed
>
> You will do this by performing a monologue and creating a social network page.

1 **Work on your own.** Read Act Two, Scene 4 to Act Three, Scene 2. Make notes about the change in Jimmy's character by this point in the play.

2 **Work in a group of three.** Imagine you are all Jimmy. However, one of you is Jimmy at the start of the play, one is Jimmy after Act Two, Scene 1, and one is Jimmy after Act Three, Scene 2. Discuss how your thoughts, feelings and emotions are different from each other.

3 **In your group**, take it in turns to talk about your thoughts, feelings and emotions as if you were Jimmy. Respond to each other's monologues and discuss the differences between them. What changes has Jimmy gone through after becoming an Angel?

4 **Work on your own.** Make a list of three characteristics that Jimmy possesses at this point in the play. For each characteristic, chose a quotation or event from the play as evidence to support it.

5 Using your knowledge of Jimmy at this point in the play, create *either* Jimmy's Facebook page or his Twitter feed over a period of time. Remember, although you should use your imagination, your ideas must be based on textual evidence.

Activity 8: Conscience walk

After reading Act Three, Scenes 3–5

You will:

- consider the decisions Jimmy makes as an Angel

You will do this by playing the role of Jimmy and going on a conscience walk.

1 **Work on your own.** Read Act Three, Scenes 3–5 carefully.

2 Make a large space within your classroom. **Work in a group of three**. One person in the group should take on the role of Jimmy, whilst two other members play Jimmy's conscience. Each group must then take it in turn to complete their conscience walk.

3 Jimmy stands at one end of the room. He can then choose to follow a path to the left or a path to the right. Left is 'Angel' and right is 'Non-Angel'. Jimmy begins to follow the path he thinks is correct at the start.

4 As Jimmy walks, the other two members of the group take the roles of Jimmy's conscience. One person whispers to Jimmy all the reasons why he should remain an Angel while the other whispers all the reasons he should not. It is up to Jimmy to decide whose voice persuades him and to walk towards his final decision. Jimmy may change direction any number of times while he decides what to do.

5 When Jimmy has reached the other end of the room, he should be at either 'Angel' or 'Non-Angel'. He must explain what helped him to make his decision.

6 Other groups should be watching the current Jimmy while he makes his walk and make note of the moments when Jimmy changes direction. What made him change his mind? Discuss these points with your group and be prepared to feed back to the class.

Activity 9: A dramatic performance

After reading Act Three, Scenes 6–7

You will:

• consider carefully the performance aspects of the play

You will do this by planning and delivering a performance of the penultimate scene of the play.

1 **Work in a group.** Read Act Three, Scenes 6–7. You will need readers for Jimmy, Sean, Ollie, Jess, Anika, Hayley and the two Voices, and one group member to be the director.

2 Imagine you were going to perform Act Three, Scene 7 for an audience at a school production of the play. Discuss how you would do this. You should consider the following:

   • how to show Jimmy's realisation that the other pupils are against him and his resulting confusion;
   • how to convey the sinister changes in the other characters;
   • what moves and actions on stage would help to build drama;
   • how you might use lights, props and sound effects to add drama to the scene as written.

3 Make a note of your group's ideas for the above points of consideration, ready to feed back to the class.

4 **Work as a class.** Each group should feed back their ideas and thoughts on how to stage the scene, discussing staging issues and how you can overcome any problems.

5 **Work in a group.** Perform the scene as effectively as you can. Then act as an audience for the other groups.

Activity 10: An extra scene

After reading Act Three, Scene 8

> You will:
> * think of a way of continuing the play after the final scene
>
> You will do this by writing a new scene for the play.

1 **Work on your own.** Read Act Three, Scene 8 carefully.

2 **Work with a partner.** Discuss any questions or thoughts an audience might have after the play has finished. Make notes about any loose ends, ambiguities, things you still want to know about characters, etc.

3 Use your notes to come up with three possible ways the action of the play could continue into a Scene 9. Explain why each idea may or may not work for an audience.

4 Agree on your best idea and a reason why you think it would be the most satisfying way to continue the play's narrative.

5 **Work on your own.** Write a new Act Three, Scene 9 for *Angels*. This should be your own version of the idea you devised in your pair. Set out your scene as a playscript, following the conventions of the original play.

6 **Work in a group.** Perform a selection of the scenes you've written and assess which one works most effectively as a way of continuing the play.

Activity 11: Pitch perfect!

After reading the play

> You will:
> * review the play
>
> You will do this by pitching an idea for the film version of the play.

1 **Work with a partner.** Discuss what makes *Angels* a moving piece of drama. Make a list of statements about what makes it so thought-provoking.

2 Devise three possible 'tag-lines' (catchy slogans that give a feel for the text) that might be used on posters or trailers to sell the film version of *Angels*.

3 **Work as a class.** Each pair should share their ideas. Discuss how you might go about adapting a play such as *Angels* for the cinema screen.

4 **Work on your own.** Would you be interested in bringing *Angels* to the big screen? Write and deliver a 'pitch' (a short, persuasive speech) aimed at a film producer to convince them this would be a great story to turn into a film.

   * The pitch must only last **one minute** when spoken and should aim to excite, enthuse and inspire.
   * Include a brief cast list of possible actors who could effectively play the roles of Jimmy, Jess, Anika and Ollie.

5 Practice your speech and deliver it to the class. You should also act as an audience for others' pitches.

6 As a class, vote on which pitch was the most convincing.

Activity 12: Storyboard

After reading the play

You will:

- decide on the key dramatic moments in *Angels*

You will do this by creating a storyboard of the play.

1 **Work in a group.** Discuss what the key dramatic moments are in the play. Think carefully about the moments that define the flow of events and meanings within the play. Choose your top six key dramatic moments.

2 Choose a line of dialogue from the play to represent each of your key moments.

3 Each group will perform their dramatic moments to the rest of the class in the form of a series of tableaux. A tableau is an arrangement of people who do not move or speak, like a freeze frame. One group member should speak the line to accompany the frozen image.

4 **Work on your own.** Present your moments in a storyboard, which is much like a comic strip. Use six boxes to draw representations of each of your six dramatic moments. Add the line of dialogue under each box.